Solo Cycling

FRED MATHENY

Solo Cycling

How to Train and Race Bicycle Time Trials

Velo-news
Brattleboro, Vermont

First printing: October 1986
Second printing: February 1987

Copyright © 1986 by Fred Matheny

Photos copyright © 1986: Tom Moran, cover; pp. 18, 37, 51, 64, 66, 105, 113, 125, 129, Michael Chritton; pp. 8, 12, 40, 56, 78, 88, 93, 161, 171, 186, 192, Robert F. George; pp. 22, 99, 135, 143, Tom Moran; pp. 26, 44, Ed Oudenaarden; pp. 71, 176, Sergio Penazzo; p. 61, courtesy of Racer-Mate; p. 21, Bernard Thompson; pp. 27, 100, 181, Cor Vos.

ISBN 0-941950-10-7

Library of Congress Catalog Card Number: 86-050910

Edited by Barbara George
Proofread by Louise Allen Zak and Marilee Attley
Typeset by The Sant Bani Press, Tilton, NH
Printed by Thomson Shore, Inc., Dexter, MI

Contents

Mind and Body and Bike

Preface

THIS BOOK tells you how to become a better time trialist – and a better all-round rider, too – using the advice of more than a dozen Olympic, world, and national championships and medalists. But I am the one who chose the riders whose tips are included. I selected which of their comments to use. I organized their advice within the framework of my own cycling experience. The result is a book that can't be separated from the personality and prejudices of the author. So it seems appropriate to begin with a note about my beginnings in the sport, my own reasons for time trialing, and my performance and expectation level. After all, if you don't know me you won't know how to judge my advice.

I began racing in 1976 in a few mass-start events and liked it, although at a muscular 175 pounds I didn't climb well. The first race I rode – Durango to Silverton, Colorado – was not the best choice because it included over 4,000 feet of vertical. Still, I was excited about my performance and decided it wasn't so bad for a 31-year-old former 205-pound collegiate football lineman. Quite a few riders outclimbed me in my inaugural race but I didn't see any who had been offensive guards.

So in January 1977 I started to train more or less seriously on the bike. For a time cycling threatened to replace all the other activities that I had previously done for enjoyment and fitness: running, basketball, skiing, weight training, mountaineering. I trimmed down to 160, got faster, and raced on the road frequently in the spring where I was successful enough to move quickly up in category. But I found it harder to make a financial commitment. I had a marginal bike with junk tires that sported an assortment of bulges, patches, and bald spots.

The first hint that I would enjoy time trials came in a road race in March. The course near Boulder was flat and windy. Fifteen miles from the finish I took a pull, looked back, and found that I had opened a gap on the field. I put my head down and kept going, too inexperienced to know that I probably had no chance in the wind against the 20 or so riders still in the pack. But they didn't know who I was and my battered bike and 'may-pop' tires didn't make me look very dangerous so they didn't chase hard until it was too late.

*A competitive high point of my 10-year career in cycling was 1981, the first year I quali-
fied for the national championships. My wife, Deb, and I made the trip from Colorado
to New York for the road and time trial events. As many years as I have been racing,
I still find excitement and satisfaction in time trialing. It's a lifelong sport that offers
both physical and mental benefits.*

I had time trialed to a two-minute lead (who is that guy?) when in
the last high-speed corner one of those long-suffering tires blew
out resoundingly and I skidded across the pavement on my side. I
was standing forlornly by the side of the road, not a spare wheel in
sight, when the pack came through, tightening their collective toestraps for the sprint. That brief glimpse of what it was like to grind
solo down the road was enough to compensate me for the loss of a
little skin, more dings on my thrift-store frame, and a sure victory
down the drain.

I am not sure what synaptic quirks of our brains make some mem-
ories, years later, remain as bright as a polished hub. Excitement,
maybe. But I still remember with an immediacy that transcends mere
recollection the feeling of knifing through the spring wind like a
shark, the smell of wet prairie grass, the fast downhill corner, and
the mountains shimmering in the background. Out there, time trialing to the finish, I seemed to have found the essence of cycling – one

rider alone and going hard. Looking back I realize that I probably hadn't found the essence of cycling at all but rather the essence of my own personality. But I couldn't see that at the time.

I rode the Colorado championship time trial that year and clocked one hour, 22 seconds. That was respectable in 1977, especially on 300-gram tires (I had put a boot in the blown one) and a bike that carried as a souvenir of that road race crash a disturbing tendency to crab sideways instead of going straight.

Also competing was legendary Colorado cyclist, and former age-group (40 and over) national champion at 25 miles, Jim Crist. I talked to him afterward and he had some words of encouragement for me, the rookie, and some advice – get some real tires.

I was hooked, and resolved to break the hour next year. I'd read somewhere that a sub-hour time for 25 miles was entry into the top ranks of time trialing. I didn't realize how devalued that time had become, even in 1978, by the rapid improvement of U.S. riders. Afire with the goal, I had the time of my mid-life trying to reach it. I trained in a more structured way, using many of the ideas in this book. I got a new bike. And I rode the early season mass-start races, again moving up in category by early summer.

In the Colorado championship time trial I cut almost two minutes off the previous year's time, turning a 58:27. That was good for sixth in the state that year, behind several national team luminaries including Tom Sain, who set a national record that day. One place ahead of me was experienced Boulder rider Tom Mereness, who six years later won the national 40km time trial title for his age group (35 to 40) with a 54:25. Fast company.

I remember a conflicting mix of emotions after that ride. I was elated at my performance, sure that I could have gone just a little faster if I had concentrated more, astounded and humbled at what Sain must have had under the hood to go three minutes faster, and full of plans to train my guts out and go even faster next year. But best of all was the sense of satisfaction at having set a goal, trained hard, and accomplished it. I've had other time trials at other distances that I consider better rides from a technical standpoint. But for sheer thrill and quantum improvement, that effort is still my best time trial memory.

That feeling of satisfaction is still the chief reason why I love time trials. After 10 years of racing, sprinkled liberally with the usual mix of highs and lows, I can still get excited about time trials even in those seasons when I'm a little blase about around-the-city-block criteriums. While I often find myself choosing to take a long solo ride in the mountains rather than driving to a 40-mile road race, I still tend to show up for time trials.

Another appeal of time trials to me is their essential simplicity. It comes down to my ability on that day to push myself into blind exhaustion. I find out while riding one, in clear and unmistakable terms, what I have inside and whether my training has gone well or badly. It is a blend of ancient and modern. As a gauge of my ability to overcome pain, it is a throwback to the initiation rites of primitive cultures. And as a test of my ability to find time for a workout in the midst of family and professional responsibilities, it is as modern as the two-career family.

In short, time trials are a simple test not just of horsepower but of how I am handling my life. This is good information to have at any time and particularly useful now when the whole process of living gets more complicated every day.

But the biggest time trial thrill is still the feeling that I had on that spring day near Boulder, the feeling of being totally engaged in an activity that requires every ounce of your strength and all of your attention. A great deal has been made recently of anaerobic threshold – a level of exertion that, if exceeded, plunges you into the oxygen debt and make you slow down or lie panting by the side of the road like a beached fish. Time trials require that you ride as close to that threshold as possible. Only in that way can you cover the distance as fast as your fitness allows. Go at a more comfortable level of work and you won't go as fast as you could. Go over that metaphorical threshold and the accumulation of waste products will waste you. You'll get into oxygen debt – blow up, in cyclists' parlance – and crawl to the finish line.

The two-edged challenge of time trialing is knowing your body so well that you can sense when you are on the edge, coupled with a steely ability to control your mind and overcome the pain so you can stay there. Time trials are a kind of athletic brinksmanship.

But there is another facet of time trialing that, for me, may be the most pleasurable of all. As I continue to race year after year I find that I don't ride many formal time trials because there aren't that many near where I live. That used to frustrate me. Now I find that it doesn't matter because another advantage of time trials is that I can do one any time I feel revved up and ready to go. I have half a dozen courses on my normal training roads, from one mile up to 41, and I have timed myself on them over the years. When I want to test my fitness I can go out and see exactly where I am – the clock doesn't lie.

A month ago I rode the 10 miles east of town to Cerro summit and did the 3.5-mile climb to the top. I have personal records on that climb going back 12 years and I broke my previous best by more than 30 seconds. It felt so good to get a PR, especially at 39, that I was fired up for two weeks and envisioned myself knocking the socks off cycling superstar Greg LeMond on every hill.

In objective terms my time probably isn't all that great. But I don't care because I have only the one standard – my previous performance – to judge myself against. If I competed against LeMond I'd be depressed and discouraged. When I compete against myself I get psyched. I didn't have to drive 250 miles to Denver to race, or plan my training especially for the event, or spend the day before the event getting nervous about it. I just climbed on the bike for a training ride, discovered that I felt good, and punched my watch at the start of the climb. Instant time trial.

Now don't get me wrong – I prefer to compete against others. But when no one else is available, the watch and my previous time are competition enough.

These are some of the reasons why time trialing is one of the most satisfying athletic events that I do. It is my hope that this book will help you share the excitement and discover your own reasons for becoming fascinated by the sport.

How do time trial champions like Ron Kiefel train and race? More than a dozen of them have been generous enough to share their advice with you in these pages.

Acknowledgements

My thanks to the following U.S. riders, coaches and mechanics who gladly offered their opinions, techniques, and unique attitudes toward time time trialing for the preparation of this book. Some of their recent achievements are listed below, and I will be quoting their comments extensively throughout the pages to come.

When Franz Hammer says that time trials are the best indication of a rider's class, he is using the word to mean inherent physical ability or, if you prefer, raw talent. But all these riders share another brand of class, too. It's the kind that prompts them to take time from the demands of training, jobs, families, and schooling to share their expertise with other riders. Their advice can help you learn quickly what they learned through long and sometimes hard experience.

They are all winners, on and off the bike.

Eddie Borysewicz (Eddie B) – U.S. Cycling Federation national coach since 1977; 1980 and 1984 U.S. Olympic team cycling coach; author, *Bicycle Road Racing*.

Ralph Brandt – 1983 Senior 35-40 national time trial championship, 2nd; 1984 5th.

Dan Casebeer – 1983-84 U.S. hour record holder (44.5km); 1984 national time trial championship, 5th; 1985 national time trial championship, 8th; 1985 national team time trial championship, 2nd.

Susan Ehlers – 1983 national time trial championship, 3rd; 1984 5th.

Franz Hammer – 1978-79 and 1981 Senior 35-45 national time trial champion; 1983-84 Senior 45-55 national road champion; 1983-85 Senior 45-50 national time trial champion; current Senior 45-50 40km record holder (56:19.6 in 1983).

Dennis Haserot – 1982 Senior 35-45 national time trial champion; 1985 Senior 35-45 national road champion and Senior 40-45 national time trial champion.

Andy Jacobs – Sports psychologist, U.S. Olympic Training Center.

Ron Kiefel – 1981-83 national team time trial champion; 1983 national road and time trial champion; 1984 Olympic team time trial, 3rd.

Roy Knickman – 1982-83 Junior national road, time trial and criterium champion; 1983 Junior world championship individual pursuit 3rd, team pursuit 2nd, team time trial 3rd; 1984 national team time trial champion; 1984 Olympic team time trial, 3rd.

Cindy Olavarri – 1983 national time trial, pursuit and kilometer champion; 1983 world pursuit championship, 2nd; 1984 national pursuit and kilometer championship, 2nd.

Andrew Paulin – 1983 national team time trial championship, 3rd; 1984 national time trial championship, 4th; 1984 national team time trial champion.

Davis Phinney – 1982-83 national team time trial champion; 1983 Pan American Games team time trial champion; 1984 Olympic team time trial, 3rd.

Ross Potoff – 1980 national team time trial championship, 3rd; 1982 Senior 35-45 national time trial championship, 2nd.

Tom Resh – 1983 national time trial championship, 6th; 1985 5th; 1985 national team time trial champion.

Deborah Shumway – 1983 national time trial championship, 2nd; 1984 7th.

John Sipay – Former USCF national team mechanic; now technical support coordinator for Campagnolo.

Rebecca Twigg – 1982 national time trial champion and world pursuit champion; 1983 national road champion; 1983 world road championship, 2nd; 1984 world pursuit champion; 1984 Olympic road race, 2nd; 1985 world pursuit champion; current U.S. record holder, 1,000 and 3,000 meters (1984).

1
What is a time trial?

*It's a test of legs and lungs
often called 'the race of truth'*

IN CYCLING, a time trial is a race in which individuals or teams cover a given course or distance alone and are ranked according to their time. In a sense, it is a race against the clock. The winner is not known until all contestants have finished and the times are compared. Similar events exist in other sports – downhill and crosscountry skiing and speedskating, for example. The qualifying laps for the Indy 500 are essentially time trials.

Contrast the time trial to the mass-start event, in cycling and in other sports. In the Boston Marathon, the Indy 500 itself, or even the Kentucky Derby the contestants all start at once and the winner is the one who crosses the finish line first. It's true that the winner also had the fastest average speed. But more than individual physical prowess may have contributed to the victory. Depending on the sport, mass-start events are also won by means of drafting, tactics, or sprinting ability.

Bicycle road racing is a case in point. It is said that drafting – riding in the slipstream of air a few feet behind another cyclist – can save as much as 15% of your energy compared to riding alone or in front. This means that in a mass-start race a rider could sit in for many miles while stronger cyclists pulled him along, then win the race with a sprint in the last 200 meters. Sprinting skill can be improved with practice, but some of this ability is inherited. Thus road racing can be extremely frustrating for the strong rider without the snap to accelerate quickly or without the sit-in-and-sprint mentality.

Team tactics play an increasingly large role in road racing, too, and often the strongest rider in the race, without a competent supporting cast, will become an also-ran. So the odds are against an individual rider, regardless of his ability, in a mass-start race.

The great appeal of time trial racing is that nearly always the strongest rider on that day wins. Of course, there are variables like punctures, mechanical troubles, or the dog taking a nap on the road. But for the most part the time trial is as good a test as there is of what you have in your legs and lungs. For this reason the time trial is often called "the race of truth."

Variety of events

There are dozens of different bicycle time trial events, and somewhere in this potpourri is probably the discipline in which you can excel. The shortest ones are held on banked tracks, called velodromes, using bicycles with only one gear and no brakes. The 1,000-meter time trial is a world championship and Olympic event that takes a top rider just over a minute. Done from a standing start in a fixed gear, it requires power, concentration, a sense of pacing, and the ability to ride through a great deal of pain for a few seconds that seem like an eternity.

Track time trials also include the individual pursuit, where two riders start on opposite sides of the track and try to catch one another. However, because the event is run for a specified distance (3,000 to 5,000 meters depending on the level of competition) and because the cyclists in most major competitions are so closely matched, to see one rider catch another is rare. So it is essentially an individual time trial. There is also a four-man version – the team pursuit – that is a marvel of precision riding and speed.

Another important track time trial is the hour record, in which a single unpaced rider goes as far as he can in 60 minutes. To hold this record is one of the most admired accomplishments in cycling. The legendary Belgian Eddy Merckx rode 49.431 kilometers in one hour in 1972 on a conventional track bike. His record stood for 12 years and was considered by some to be unassailable since it had cost Merckx, perhaps the greatest racer of all time, so much pain and suffering. Then in 1984, using a more aerodynamic bicycle with disk wheels, Italian pro Francesco Moser startled the racing world with 51.151 kilometers.

The longest time trials are also record attempts, but on the road. The current ultimate in the U.S. is the 3,000-mile Race Across America. In 1985 Jonathan Boyer made the trip from Huntington

Beach, CA, to Atlantic City, NJ, in nine days, two hours and six minutes – a new transcontinental record.

In Europe, the center of world professional racing, time trials are frequently held as part of stage races like the Tour de France. The Tour lasts three weeks with separate events, called stages, held each day. The winner is the rider with the shortest combined time for all the stages, which are mostly mass-start road races lasting up to seven hours. Time trial stages can alter the outcome dramatically, however. The calculating cyclist can ride defensively in the road stages, then ring up big time margins in the stages against the clock. French organizers of the Tour have often been accused of planning the format of the race to include strategically placed time trials that benefit French riders. In 1985 Greg LeMond became the first U.S. male rider ever to win a stage of the Tour de France, when he took the 21st stage, a 45km time trial.

Two of Europe's most famous time trials are held each fall – the classic Grand Prix of Nations in France and the Baracchi Trophy in Italy – and they feature some of the best pros in the world. Five-time Tour de France winner Bernard Hinault has won the 89km hilly GP of Nations four times. LeMond was second in 1983, the same year he won the world road championship. The Baracchi Trophy is a two-man event, covering 96 kilometers. Winners in 1985 were Moser and amateur hour record holder Hans Henrik Oersted. LeMond and teammate Hinault were seventh.

The typical time trial

What is the typical time trial like? The kind I will mostly be describing in this book is 10-40 kilometers, held on an out-and-back course. That is, you go to a certain point – half the distance – turn around at a marker, come back the same way you went out, and finish where you started. Contestants start at one-minute intervals. For the start, you are already astride your bike with toestraps tightened. An official holds your bike in place from behind until you get the signal to start.

If you should happen to overtake the rider who started ahead of you – called your minute man – you are not supposed to take shelter in his slipstream (drafting) but must stay a certain distance away, even while passing. At the halfway point – or turnaround, as it is called – someone will probably write down your number to verify that you did cover the complete distance. At the finish your

The 1,000-meter time trial on the track is an Olympic and world championship event for amateur men. From a standing start it takes a little more than a minute of flat-out effort.

time is recorded. When everyone has finished and their elapsed times are calculated the standings can be announced.

If the event is held under the auspices of the governing body of the amateur sport – the U.S. Cycling Federation – you must have a USCF license to enter. (See appendix for how to get one.) Rules for USCF events are stricter than most local club races. Your clothing (including helmet) and bicycle must meet certain requirements. Drafting rules are very specific (see appendix) and violations carry penalties.

The USCF maintains U.S. records, both road and track. Since 1975 it has held district (state) and national road time trial championships. From 1975 to 1982 the championship distance was 25 miles. In '83 it became 40km (24.86 miles) for Seniors (over 18 years old) and 20km for Juniors. There are separate events for men and women in various age groups. To compete in the nationals in the individual time trial you must qualify in your district. There are no qualification standards for the 100km team time trial, which became a national championship event in 1980. Your team of four riders must register in advance. At least three of you must finish, because the time of the team is taken on the third rider.

The USCF or local club time trial appears to be patterned on the British model. Time trialing is particularly popular in England, though it apparently wasn't a consciously developed branch of cycling but rather grew out of necessity. At the turn of the century, so the story goes, mass-start road racing on the dusty carriage paths of the day was posing a real threat to pedestrians and horses alike. Police intervened again and again, often citing the whole field at the end of a race. In one famous encounter the police reportedly strung a cable across the road, wiping out a whole pack of riders and causing one fatality. Apocryphal or not, incidents like these eventually led to the banning of mass-start road racing on public roads.

Time trialing was established to get around this legality. Because riders started one minute apart and were racing the clock instead of each other, what they were doing was technically legal. To avoid the police, for whom the distinction was hazy at best, British time trials started at dawn, the races were on lightly traveled back roads, and riders wore black tights and long-sleeved woolen jackets, supposedly to make them less conspicuous. Some clubs went so far as to identify the various courses by secret codes known only to club members. In spite of these clandestine trappings, the sport boomed and still retains its popularity in England even though road racing was legalized after World War II and black jackets have gone the way of leather cleats.

Some reasons to try it

Unless you are a recreational (or non-USCF) rider or a full-time triathlete, it is very unlikely that your only cycling competition will be time trials. For one thing, there is not enough time trial racing in the U.S. to satisfy the avid competitor. But even if mass-start racing is your major interest, time trialing offers some unique attractions. Age is less of a handicap, for example. The added years may rob older riders of some oxygen uptake, but seem to compensate with greater experience and ability to suffer.

Time trialing is an ideal form of competition for the rider who usually trains alone. The training principle of specificity says, not surprisingly, that your body will perform better at tasks that you practice. Relatively few riders have a compatible group to train with frequently. You may live in an area isolated from the centers of competition or you may find that the scheduled time for the local group ride is inconvenient. Or perhaps you don't like the danger of all those bikes around you ridden by people whose attention may wander, whose skills are suspect, whose front tires may blow out without warning. For all these reasons, many serious riders in this country ride alone most of the time and that training pattern is best suited to time trials.

Time trials are also the best competitive choice for riders who dislike interval training and other forms of anaerobic workouts but who like to ride steadily near their anaerobic threshold. This kind of training has plenty of advantages. It is less painful, so you can look forward to your ride rather than dreading it. Also, steady rides are the best form of overall cardiovascular conditioning, so the daily general workout you use to maintain health and fitness doubles as your training for competition. You are free to pedal at a level of work that allows your mind to float, liberated by the rhythmic movement. Of course, to really excel in time trials, you have to do some speed-work. But you can time trial quite well without doing intervals too often or by doing non-structured types of speed training.

Another advantage of time trials: They allow riders with widely differing body types to succeed. Most time trial courses are relatively flat, so a big powerful rider who may have difficulty climbing can do well. Cycling and running are two of the best lifetime sports for the development of cardiovascular fitness and the associated health benefits. Yet many people who need aerobic training the most are large-framed athletes – former football players, for instance – who are too big-boned and muscular to run well. When they switch to the bike, they get passed on long climbs, much to their disgust, by small riders built like marathon runners. They get frustrated, see themselves as failures, and take up tennis or dedicated loafing. Yet these same athletes can be deadly in flatter time trials where their power can be used to its maximum advantage.

But you don't have to be a physical demon to ride time trials well. One unique aspect of the event is that you can be successful using a wide variety of approaches. Some riders are fast because of brute power, while others finesse the event, using a fast cadence and a supple pedaling style.

The official who holds you at the line is not supposed to either restrain or push you, but merely lets go. This is the two-mile prologue time trial of the Tour of Britain, a 12-day stage race.

The event's appeal to the generalist means that training for it can allow you to get fit for other sports. The steady-state training of bicycle time trials carries over into the long endurance events. A summer of time trialing will get you in great shape for crosscountry skiing. Quite a few mountain runners here in Colorado ride the bike for part of their training because it builds iron quadriceps.

Interested in triathlons? The cycling leg is a time trial. Many triathletes use their local time trial as the center of a once-weekly race simulation workout by swimming a half mile, riding the local TT, then running home. Timed correctly, and with someone at the time trial to pick up their bike, they can practice transitions as well as the actual event.

Another reason to consider time trials is their availability. They are easy to promote, requiring little organization and few people to run. Simple ones can be done with just one non-rider: someone who holds the watch and records times. You don't even need a holder if

Developing your time trial skills can pay off in a mass-start road race. A solo break-away may be your best chance to win, especially if sprinting is not your strong point.

everyone starts with one foot down or holds onto the fender of a car parked just off the road. In fact, you can put on your own time trials on any suitable stretch of road. If only one other person shows up, you still have competition. And if you give a time trial and no one else comes, you can still compete against your previous best.

Time trials are appealing for less concrete reasons, too. They have a built-in numerical magic like the four-minute mile or the three-hour marathon. Riders strive to break the hour for 25 miles, or ride a 10-miler in under 24 minutes (25 m.p.h.). This quantitative factor allows you to be more precise than you can be in road racing when you compare your performance to other riders and to your previous best. In road racing, two different 50-mile races on the same course may be fast one day and five minutes slower the next, due to tactics and the way the race unfolds. Time trials appeal to the quantitative mind because you can get a good idea of how you did based on numbers.

TTs help road racers
Time trials are the perfect entry-level event for eventual mass-start racing. The nightmare of every rookie rider is to get unceremoniously dropped on the first lap of a race while friends and spectators look on in polite silence. But if you don't have any race

experience and you rarely have the opportunity to train with the riders you'll be competing against, how do you know if you have what it takes? Ride some time trials and see how your times stack up against those of experienced competitors. Then you'll know better if you can start road racing with a reasonable degree of success, or if you need to spend more training time developing power and speed.

Even if you are an experienced road or criterium racer, time trial training and racing can help you get better in mass-start events. Quite a few hard-core roadies profess to hate time trials, calling them boring because they don't require the skills and tactics of mass-start racing and, because of the requirement for continual hard effort, too painful. But the fact is that any road racer who wants to excel needs to have top time trial power.

European cycling legend Jacques Anquetil won most of his five Tour de France victories on the basis of his time trial ability. Anquetil did not have blinding speed but he had plenty of power and was incredibly tenacious. This enabled him to stay with the leaders in the road stages, even though he could rarely win if it came to a sprint. Then he gained enough time in the individual time trials to win the overall general classification. It was said of Anquetil that though he never dropped anyone, no one ever dropped him. The comment reflects the grudging admiration that flashy sprinters often have for the kind of power they lack and which regular time trialing builds.

Of course, road races are themselves often a series of time trials. Many races are won on solo breaks by riders who distrust their chances in a bunch sprint, but have confidence in their ability to time trial alone to the victory. Rebecca Twigg, who can do it all — sprint, climb, and time trial — calls solo efforts like this "one way to win a race." She demonstrated her savvy in the Colorado National Monument stage of the 1983 Coors Classic, America's version of the Tour de France. Twigg escaped from her break companions, two future world road champions, on a twisting descent and time trialed 10 miles to win by a minute and a half.

Sometimes a break will go and you'll miss it. If you are caught halfway back in the pack when several top riders vanish up the road, the race is over for you unless you have the time trial power to bridge the gap. The same is true if you puncture or crash and have to chase. If you can't get back on, the best sprint in the world is useless. LeMond demonstrated this ability early in his career at the 1977 Junior national road championship. He crashed twice but was able to get up, rejoin the pack, and win the sprint at the end.

Even in the shelter of the pack, time trialing power is important, especially in team tactics. For instance, the 7-Eleven team is probably the most successful team in the country — primarily because of patented tactics. With several laps to go, one of their strongmen will go to the front and pull the pack at high speed, using his time trial power to make everyone suffer and spread the bunch out into a thin line. In the mayhem a top sprinter like Davis Phinney will move up into position so at the last corner he can use his speed to blow everyone else away. Riders and spectators alike are amazed at Phinney powering out of the corner in 53x12 and flying to the line. Only the most knowledgeable viewer realizes that it was his teammate's time trial-like effort at the front that put Davis on the victory stand.

Interested? In the rest of this book, I'll show you how top riders like Phinney, Twigg, and others prepare for, ride, and win time trials.

2
Your position and bike
*The aim is comfort, efficiency
and a streamlined profile*

BEFORE YOU CAN hope to reach your physical potential as a time trialist, you need a bike that fits and a position on that bike that makes you as streamlined and biomechanically efficient as possible. There are several approaches for finding the bicycle frame size that will work best for you. The general rule is to use as small a frame as possible because smaller frames are lighter, stiffer, and more responsive than large ones.

Many riders, some of them quite experienced, are on frames that are too large. You probably don't need one as big as you think — that is why seatposts are made long. For instance, I know of a top international stage racer who is 6-foot-5 with long legs. Yet his custom racing bike's seat tube length is only 62cm or 24.4 inches. Compare this to many beginning 6-foot riders who end up with 24-inch frames and wonder why they can't get their position right. On that tall rider's bike there is a lot of seatpost showing and the stem is long but all is in proportion right down to the 180cm cranks.

I am 5-foot-11 with a crotch-to-sole measurement of 88cm and I feel comfortable on a 56cm frame. Moser, who has the same leg length and is about one inch taller than I am uses a similar-sized frame with a longer stem extension to accommodate his longer arms and torso. And there is room for a little variation, too. American pro Boyer is also 5-foot-11 but uses a 58cm frame.

Of course the best way to find the right size frame for you is to ride a number of different ones over the years. That is why most experienced riders generally look comfortable on their bikes. Another method is to get a frame custom built and have the frame builder measure you so the bike is a perfect fit.

Those two approaches can bankrupt a sheik so most riders use some cookbook methods that work just as well. One alternative available at most pro bike shops is the Fit Kit, designed by long-

You don't have to have a special bike to maintain a low position and flat back, as these two photos of Greg LeMond show. Here, in the '86 Tour de France which he won, LeMond uses an aerodynamic time trial bike with sloping top tube, rear disk wheel, and a radially spoked front wheel.

time racer Bill Farrell. The shop personnel take several measurements on you, then use charts in the Fit Kit to determine your best frame size, stem and top tube combination, handlebar width, and crank size. Farrell developed the system by measuring hundreds of top riders and their bikes to see why good racers look so classy when they ride. These measurements served as a basis for the figures in the Fit Kit. Some shops also have a Serotta Size-Cycle, a bicycle frame completely adjustable in size. By sitting on it you can, in effect, try out many different frame sizes, saddle positions, and stem lengths.

So if a shop near you has either of these ingenious tools, it is

Even on a more traditional road bike, as here in the '86 Tour of Switzerland, LeMond can maintain the wind-cheating profile that saves valuable energy in solo riding.

worth the reasonable fee to be sure you're getting the right size bike. Even experienced racers have afterthoughts. Every winter in the racing publications the classified ads list a dozen bikes for sale with the notation "Nearly new, wrong size." Don't make a $500 mistake.

Saddle height

Once you have the correct frame size, the key to a good position on the bike is saddle height. The traditional method of determining it is to sit on the saddle with your heels flat on the pedals. If you can pedal backwards without rocking your hips on the saddle you are in the ball park. However, thinking in this area is changing because of some physiological tests done on experienced riders measuring power output at various saddle heights. A European pro team also did some tests and found that efficiency is improved if the saddle is raised as much as 2-3cm above the standard height.

Olympic gold medalist Connie Carpenter reported that she raised her saddle 3cm before the 1983 season. She not only had good results but the change alleviated some nagging knee problems. When riders attending training camps at the Olympic Training Center are checked for position by the coaching staff their saddles are often raised above the position they have been using.

Even among European pros in the 1960s, when a low saddle position was standard, Anquetil favored a higher saddle than most of his peers. He also pedaled with his toes pointed downward, an aberration unheard of at the time. Interestingly enough, Moser also pedals with pointed toes, a style he says he uses naturally, not because of a conscious effort to imitate Anquetil.

Many riders today have resisted the move to lofty saddle heights and still go by the traditional heels-on-the-pedal measurement because they feel that they can get more power into the stroke in this way. Typical is the comment of Ross Potoff who checks his position using this method. He argues that "as long as my butt doesn't shift from side to side and my heels don't come off the pedals, that's my ideal height."

If you haven't found your most efficient position through experience my suggestion is to start with the heel-on-the-pedal technique and see how you feel. Under no circumstances should your saddle be lower. If it feels uncomfortable, raise the saddle no more than ⅛ inch a week until you feel that you are reaching for the pedals, then back down a bit. All of this is tremendously individual, which is why so many riders swear by one saddle height or another.

If you pedal with your toes pointing down, you'll need a higher saddle than a rider who pedals flatfooted. And don't make the mistake of trying to change your pedaling style just because you think you need a higher saddle. In this situation, your body usually knows best. The size of your feet influences saddle height, too, as does the distance your shoe goes into the toeclip. So make any changes gradually, always noting them in your training diary so you can judge the effects on your performance and your tendons.

Foot position

The next variable is the fore and aft position of your foot on the pedal. This is adjusted by moving your cleats and possibly changing the length of the toeclips. The standard rule is to have the ball of your foot directly over the pedal spindle and this seems to work for most riders. If too much of your foot is in the toeclip, you'll have a flatfooted, ungainly pedaling style. If you are too much on your toes you may not be able to generate much power. Also, the increased leverage seems to aggravate knee or Achilles tendon problems in some riders. I like to be slightly on my toes (i.e., have the ball of my foot a bit behind the pedal spindle) but that is the way I run and my legs seem to be built that way.

Choose toeclips after you've found the correct foot position, not before. Be sure there is a little room between the front of the shoe and clip or the metal will rub on your toes and you may lose a toenail. Runners with tight shoes and cyclists with tight toeclips both get black toenails.

Cleat adjustment

Perhaps the most crucial adjustment in an orthopedic sense is the lateral position of your foot on the pedal. If you toe in or toe out too much, the strain of that unnatural angle will get transferred directly to your knee with painful results. It's probably safe to say that most minor cases of sore knees as well as full-blown tendinitis stem from improperly adjusted cleats.

The best way to make sure your cleats are adjusted correctly is to get them checked on the Rotational Adjustment Device in Farrell's Fit Kit. The RAD determines the natural position of your feet on the pedals. Then the cleats are adjusted to let you maintain it. It allows you to pedal in the position that your unique foot, knee, and lower leg configuration wants you to. The traditional way of checking this was to ride for several days in cycling shoes without cleats and then mount the cleat parallel to the line imprinted by the pedal cage on the leather sole of the shoe. Today nearly all cycling shoes come with premounted adjustable cleats so that solution is impractical.

If you don't have access to a Fit Kit, check your normal foot alignment by walking on dry cement in wet feet and looking at the pattern. If you toe in slightly when you walk, it's a pretty good bet that you'll need to toe in slightly on the pedal to avoid knee problems. This sounds like an unscientific if not downright haphazard method of checking something as important as foot position. But it seems to work.

For instance, cyclists who ride behind me are amazed that anyone can pedal at all with the pigeon-toed style I have. The inside rear corner of the cleats on my Duegis are moved as far as they will go to the inside of the shoe and my heels are more than an inch from the crankarm. But people who walk behind me are amazed too. My tracks in the snow look like my shoes are talking to each other as they walk. Yet I don't have knee trouble with this position (knock on wood) and it has been checked out on the Fit Kit and lines right up. So find out what works for you.

Fore/aft saddle position

With saddle height and foot position arranged correctly, the next step is to determine saddle fore and aft position. Again a standard rule: With the cranks horizontal and your foot in normal pedaling position, a plumb line dropped from your knee should bisect the pedal spindle. To position the plumb line, first locate the bony bump below your kneecap called the tibial tuberosity. Hold the plumb line just below the tibial tuberosity.

Be aware that this puts most riders more forward on the bike than they may be used to riding. In fact, short-thighed riders may have to push the saddle nearly all the way forward on the seatpost to get it right. Even then some riders can't do it unless they have a bike with very upright seat tube angles. European pros usually have their saddles back, believing that a more stretched-out position is better for long races on rough pavement or with extensive climbing. But a forward position enables you to get power into the pedal stroke in time trials because your weight and strength are above the pedal in the power part of the stroke.

If you tend to slide forward on the saddle when you are pedaling hard and fast, like in an all-out jam, your saddle may be adjusted incorrectly. Most riders sit on the tip of the saddle a little when they're giving it their all but that's a very inefficient and tiring position for a longer event like a time trial.

Saddle tilt

Finally, adjust the top of the saddle so that it's nearly dead level. Do this by placing a yardstick on top of the saddle and checking its alignment in relation to the top tube. Many male riders like the tip slightly elevated while most women find this very uncomfortable.

Saddle model makes a difference too. Some of the highbacked saddles like the Concor have a fairly pronounced dip in the center. This means the tip can irritate you even when the saddle is level. The incorrect saddle for your body configuration is a guarantee of discomfort, saddle sores, and numb crotch. So don't be afraid to experiment with various models. Many experienced riders have a closet full of saddles they have tried and rejected, so ask around.

Stem length

Okay, your saddle is adjusted correctly and your feet are where they should be. The rest is easy — just find a stem that is the right length. It is traditional to choose a stem by getting into time trialing position with your hands on the drops and then glancing down at the front hub. If the front of the stem and the handlebars obscure the hub the stem length is basically correct.

Many time trialists favor a slightly longer stem because it stretches them out more over the bike and aids their aerodynamic position. Don't carry this too far. Long stems do get you low and aerodynamic but, as Farrell says of bikes set up that way, "You still have to pedal the thing." And Olympic gold medalist Alexi Grewal says that his rule for stem position is "lower and shorter."

Your stem length will vary between frames depending on the top tube length, too. I have two 56cm frames but the top tube on one is 55cm while the other is 56. To get an identical position on the two bikes, I need stems 1cm different in length.

One way to get a consistent position from bike to bike is to measure the distance from saddle tip to handlebar center on the bike you feel best on. Then try to duplicate the measurement on your other bikes (as long as they use the same saddle). This can be done for saddle height, too, by measuring from the bottom bracket center to the top of the saddle in line with the seat tube.

Stem height

Stem height is another area where you will have to experiment. Long-armed riders with long torsos generally have a low handlebar position, sometimes putting the stem into the head tube almost as far as it will go regardless of the the amount of seatpost they have showing. This can give them a differential between the top of the bars and the top of the saddle of five inches or more.

Stocky riders find that a low handlebar position cramps their breathing and makes their thighs hit against their ribs on each pedal stroke. Also, time trialing uses big gears. You need the power of your back in each stroke, power that comes more naturally from a slightly upright position. Find a balance between aerodynamics and biomechanics.

Cheating the wind

As you can see, the way you choose your stem length and height has a lot to do with your position on the bike. And that in turn strongly influences your time. Riders spend a couple months of paychecks for fancy aerodynamic equipment and then negate all those advantages by presenting a broad frontal profile to the wind.

Look at a rider and bike from the front. Notice how little frontal area the bike has and how large the rider looms, no matter how tight his position may be. Time trialing is a wind-cheating event. If your position is faulty and you end up catching a lot of air with your chest and arms no amount of aerodynamic equipment will help. The wind will win.

Some riders take a chance and adjust their normal riding positions for time trials. Former national team mechanic John Sipay supports such changes, saying they are the single best thing you can do to reduce wind resistance. "Get as far down as you can comfortably," he says. "You have a wonderful thing that allows you to get low. It's called bending your elbows." In addition, many European pros assume a different position on their special time trial bikes than they would on a regular road bike. But in general, for most riders, the standard road position is best. "The position that is best for me on the road," says Cindy Olavarri, "is also best in time trials."

You need to develop a good position and practice it each time you go out training. "Position isn't something that comes in a week or two weeks," says Sipay. "It's a constant reminder. Like any training, the results don't come overnight." This doesn't mean that you have to ride every minute of every training ride on the drops. But when you go hard – as in intervals, repeat work, or training time trials – use your racing position, experimenting to get it right.

It's also a good idea to have pictures taken of you while you ride. The easiest way to do that is to have someone take them with a Polaroid camera while you are riding a windload simulator or rollers. You can check the pictures almost immediately, try different positions, and see which look and feel the best. You may think your position is as aerodynamic as a cruising shark when actually you are a bit upright. A picture won't lie.

What should that position look like? For flat or rolling time trials your hands should be on the drops. Your elbows should be tucked in slightly so they don't ride along outside the profile of your body and create drag. Keep your head up so you can look down the road and see obstacles in front of you. The whole idea is to stay low and present as small a frontal area to the wind as possible while still being able to breathe comfortably. A good time trialist looks very similar in profile to a downhill skier tucked into what is called the egg position.

Keep back flat

One way to facilitate an aerodynamic position is to keep your back flat. Coaches like Eddie Borysewicz at the Olympic Training Center emphasize the flat back ad nauseum and riders who have trained there have heard this coaching point over and over. Twigg, who has a stylish position on the bike in time trials on both road and track, says, "Eddie B keeps saying flatten your back. I have a long upper body and short legs so it looks like I'm low but Eddie always bothers me about keeping a flat back."

In fact, this coaching point has been emphasized so often in recent years that some riders have overdone it, arching their backs until they look like the old gray mare and then wondering why they get excruciatingly sore in the lower back muscles when they compete or train hard. Use a little horse sense.

Another negative result of too flat a back is that the resulting extremely low position can make it difficult to breathe. You don't want your thighs coming up and banging your lower ribs and diaphragm to such an extent that your ability to get that oxygen in and out is compromised. Dan Casebeer, who processed quite a bit of oxygen on his way to the U.S. hour record, cautions: "It is important to have good breathing. So don't bind yourself up with a position that is too low."

Another problem is that a very low, stretched-out position makes it difficult to get the strength of your lower back and arms into the stroke. Dennis Haserot says that after a time trial his arms are as tired as his legs. Climbing requires a lot of power and good climbers sit up and hold onto the tops of the bars so they can use their whole bodies to generate the power they need. Of course, they don't have to worry about wind resistance because of the slower speeds at which climbing is done. So you don't want to ride a flat time trial sitting up and pulling on the bars since the additional power would be negated by the added wind resistance.

On the other hand, you'll often see pictures of top European pros, in time trials or on solo breaks in road races, cranking along in 53x13 with their hands on the tops next to the stem in what looks like a climbing position. They do this when the road slants up slightly for 200 meters or when there is a gusty little headwind. The added power helps them over the hard spot and they think that it negates the temporary wind resistance. Notice too that, although their hands are on the tops of the bars, their body position is still low.

What all this comes down to is that you have to find a good compromise. It should be something between a radically low position with your nose on the stem – a position that may steal your power and ability to breathe freely – and an upright position that may be good for riding a mountain bike uphill. This position will vary for different riders because of their body structures.

Good vision

One other concern is safety. A low position makes it difficult to look very far down the road because you have to hold your head up in an unnatural way and your neck muscles can fatigue quickly. This is devastating to your performance because the stress and fatigue of the neck muscles will spread until your whole upper body tightens up. But it is vital to find a position that lets you have an unobstructed visual shot at the road ahead. If you have trouble with fatigue in your neck and trapezius muscles, do exercises with a neck harness that is available from sporting goods dealers. This will also strengthen the muscles that protect your spinal column in the neck in the event of a crash. For more on the subject, see the chapter on weight training.

Good vision is even more important in training than racing since you have so many more opportunities to get nailed. Potoff, who has had more experience tangling with cars than he cares to remember, says, "I don't always employ a good aerodynamic style in training because of external elements like vehicular traffic. After being hit a few times I have the tendency to be a little more safety-conscious."

3
Setting goals
Success and failure are relative;
it's up to you to define them

THEY MATERIALIZE every season, that year's acknowledged hot-
shots, destined to break the hour in their first 40-kilometer time
trial and rise through the USCF rider categories like hot air bal-
loons. At every race they take places from the pluggers who would
trade their De Rosas for enough top-six finishes to advance in category.

I remember one of these comers from several seasons ago. He had
a motor, coupled with the desire to work hard. He had enough
mechanical aptitude to keep his bike working. In time trials he
blasted by everyone full tilt but always seemed to have something
left. In mass-start races a fine blend of aggressiveness and relaxation took him through tight corners or to the front for the sprint
with equal aplomb. His parents were eager to support him finan-
cially and emotionally in the sport. In short, he had talent in all its
aspects.

He was eighth at a big race in his first season of competition
against national riders – all the heavies. He was beaten in the
sprint from lack of experience but he had been there the whole time,
climbing with the leaders and taking his pulls on the flat.

I congratulated him afterward but he was downcast. He shrugged
off my encouragement and eyed the victor who was wearing the red,
white and blue jersey of national champion and had ridden with an
air of studied nonchalance.

"I want to get good," my acquaintance said in response to my encouragement. I was given to understand that "good" meant not just
tough in Colorado but national caliber, not merely strong but over-
powering. Like heroes of myth he wanted divine help, Medusa's
head to turn his opponents' legs to stone, talent not merely dominat-
ing but supernatural.

He hasn't raced since that year. I haven't seen him to ask why, but I know. He was a victim of inflated goals, of unreasonable expectations, of being too good too fast on the strength of natural ability. He didn't know how to improve past the place where his natural ability could take him.

Of course, there isn't any mystical path to improvement. It takes hard work. But, more than that, it takes a calculated, informed plan to guide you in deciding how and when to do that work.

How can you get good? Let's look at the steps you need to take to improve your time trial performance and general cycling ability. And if you don't have the sort of inherited talent that the Colorado hotshot had, don't despair. These principles can help anyone who wants better results at any level of competition.

Six principles

It all starts with a plan. It is important to have a schedule mapped out for each week of training as well as for the whole year. A comprehensive schedule tells you not only what you should do on a given day but also how that day's training fits into your goals for a season and for your whole cycling life. Without one, your training will be aimless.

Assuming that you begin the process of developing your schedule in the winter, the first step is to set your goals for the coming year. Every rider is different. Your goal may be to use the bike to become fit, to better this year's time in the local time trial, to do well in a major triathlon, or to win the nationals. Regardless of the height of your ambitions, base your goal setting on these principles.

1. *Know yourself.* Only you know what you want to get out of cycling. You alone know how much psychological capital you can afford to invest in the stress of training and racing. And you are the best judge of your training load – how much will make you better, how much more will break you down.

2. *How much time can you train?* Your goals should be related to how much time you are willing to spend to reach them. If you are heavily involved in studies, have a family, a full-time job, or all of the above, chances are you'll have little energy left over for training intensely. And it isn't just training time that you need. Recovery is at least as important. Working nine to five, whether on your feet at a retail sales job or at your desk solving the problems of the world, isn't recovery time.

The best racers do nothing but eat, sleep, train, and recover. You probably don't have that kind of time to devote to the sport. Quite

Whether you aim to place high in an important event or simply to improve your 40km time by a few seconds, you need season-long goals to shape your training plan.

possibly you don't want to live and breathe cycling. Don't set goals that are impossible to reach within the parameters of the rest of your life.

One season I was even more enthused about racing than usual because I had some encouraging results in early events. Busy with my family, teaching, and some evening meetings I usually had to train at 5:30 or 6:00 a.m. I would grab a little breakfast at school before class and recover from a hard 40-miler while striding around the room helping students with their work or leading the class through the intricacies of John Milton's *Paradise Lost*. It didn't work, of course, and after a month I was so tired that my race results got worse and worse.

With hindsight I can see that I would have had more success doing less training and more recovering. As it was, I never improved because I got too tired. My good early results, which I thought were just the beginning, turned out to be the best I did all season. Paradise lost.

Everyone knows that top racers, amateur or pro, are at the sport full-time. But I've always been fascinated by the fact that many of the best older competitors — the ones in the 35-and-up age group — have flexible schedules that allow them to train when they want. Some are self-employed, with businesses that run themselves for a few hours each day while they ride. If you aren't in that situation, set your goals accordingly and don't make the mistake I did of trying to get 26 hours' worth of living into a 24-hour day.

3. *Have a plan.* When you go on a trip, you have a map. When you attend a meeting, you're provided with an agenda. When you grease your bottom bracket, you follow clearly defined and ordered steps. So when you train, have a plan. Decide how many events you can ride and which ones are most important. It is foolish to do intense training all year when you'll only be riding four or five local time trials. By the same token, why do sharpening work like motorpacing in March if the race you really want to win is in August? You have a limited amount of energy. Wise training choices will enable you to use it when it will do the most good.

4. *Include variety.* If you are on a trip and there is a bridge washed out, you look at your map and choose from other options. If you go out for a scheduled hard ride on Tuesday and you feel tired and washed out, look at your training plan and choose from a variety of easier workouts. Goals are easier to reach if you alter your training frequently.

The body and mind both need variety and crave a change of scene. You probably get plenty of sameness in your job or your surroundings or in your circle of friends. Why continue the pattern in your training? Training is supposed to be recreation. Re-create. Why do the same intervals week after week? The same squat routine? Or, God help you, the same routine on the rollers every day from November to March looking out the same window at the same neighbor's snowy front yard listening to the same Stones tape?

5. *Train for success.* Set your goals in small, attainable increments so you can reach them. If you rode a two-mile training time trial in five minutes, set your goal for next week at 4:58. Don't set it at 4:45. You probably won't make it, and then what? You've been training for failure.

Success or failure in time trialing are relative terms. You can define what they mean for you. So define them in such a way that you'll achieve small but significant successes each day. Success breeds more and bigger success but failure breeds only failure and frustration until finally you are fed up with the sport.

6. *Use your carefully orchestrated successes to build a winner's self concept.* You are what you believe you are. If you think that you are going to win, you have a much better chance of doing so. Most pre-race prophecies are self-fulfilling whether for good or bad.

Did you ever hear of the Hawthorne effect? Researchers took three classrooms of school children with identical ability as revealed by a pre-test and they instructed three teachers how to teach each class during the year. On opening day, the first teacher went into her class and said "I've looked at your test results. You are a below-average class so I have very few expectations. We'll struggle along through the material as best we can." And she proceeded to teach that way.

The second teacher told his class, "The test showed that you are all about average. I have average expectations for you, I'll assign a normal work load, and I expect average work." And that is how he taught.

The third teacher entered her class with her eyes glowing. "Never in all my years of teaching has it been my privilege to have students with the ability that you have. We are going to work very hard, I'll expect top-quality work, but I know you are capable."

At the end of the year the three classes (that had tested the same in September) were retested. The first class scored below the norm, the second class was about average, and the third class blew the top off the scale. Moral: We are what we expect to be. We perform the way significant others expect us to perform.

Obviously, a rider who hasn't trained properly isn't going to set records just because he thinks he is unbeatable. He has to train hard and long even if he has good natural ability to start with. But that is just the point: Well-trained time trialists are so similar in their physical ability that how they think about the race often determines the winner. Remember, too, that someone who doesn't expect to win when the racing begins is unlikely to do the sort of high-quality training in the months leading up to competition. You have a choice, so choose to train for success, not for failure.

Olympic and national cycling coach Eddie Borysewicz uses the scheduling method called periodization in training the national team. The result has been more than 50 international medals for U.S. amateurs since 1978.

4
The training plan
*Build power and fitness gradually
with a year-round program*

ONCE YOU'VE identified your goals for the season, how do you translate them into specific training schedules for time trialing? I suggest that you adopt the kind of year-long training program that has worked for many of the top cyclists in the U.S. and Europe. This scheduling method, called periodization, is used by U.S. Olympic and national coach Eddie Borysewicz for the national team. Part of it comes from principles that are used in other sports. It is not rigid but amenable to endless variation. I'll outline the various components in this chapter. If some of the terms are unfamiliar or you don't know exactly how to do some of the workouts, don't worry. I'll explain the details in subsequent chapters. But first, an overview.

Periodization

The widely used scheduling technique called periodization divides the year into sections with a definite training plan for each one. The idea is to work on all aspects of racing fitness and technique during the year, building power and aerobic fitness over long periods of time and then sharpening up with racing and fast training for planned peak performances.

Most riders divide the year roughly into the following periods:
1. Preparation – October, November, December
2. Pre-season – January, February, March
3. Competitive season – April through September

The preparation period is a time to do activities other than cycling, especially if you raced the previous season. After an intense competitive summer you need to get away from the bike for a physical and psychological rest.

Don't underestimate the psychological benefits of forgetting about cycling for awhile. Potoff lives in Arizona where you can ride all year. That may sound great if you come from Minnesota but, as he points out, it has a negative side. "It is not very difficult to get totally saturated with riding if you train seriously year-round," Potoff says. "I've see hundreds of decent riders get burned out after only a few seasons."

Ron Kiefel had a very succesful season in 1983, including an unprecedented three gold medals in the national road championships (individual road race, time trial and team time trial). What does a rider like that do in the winter? After such an intense competitive season, Kiefel says, "I keep active as much as possible. I go to school to keep my brain active and let my body recover. I do circuit training, uphill running, Turbo Trainer, cyclocross, mountain bike and exercise class. I try to mix it up as much as possible." Active rest and a change of pace is the idea.

Different activities will help develop your all-round athletic skills. Cycling is a very specialized sport and the sad fact is that some very fast riders have been extremely poor general athletes. A little winter involvement in sports that require some eye-hand coordination and body control can make a big difference in summer cycling when you have to circle the turnaround cone or dodge an errant dog. National team members do tumbling drills all winter, for example, to help them if they crash.

Don't feel that you aren't improving during this preparation period. The rejuvenating effect of different activities sets the stage for specific improvement in cycling later in the year. Also, varied activities stimulate overall strength improvement. Phinney maintains that his time trialing "has improved primarily through years of consistent off-season training and in-season riding and racing." You can't have one without the other.

During the preparation period you should also have a complete physical exam by a sports-oriented physician, preferably one experienced with cyclists or other endurance athletes. If you are just getting started in the sport the check will uncover any abnormalities that might limit your success. If you raced hard last season, appropriate blood tests and other checks can spot deficiencies that still linger from the rigors of competition. A positive checkup will give you the peace of mind to begin the more strenuous training of the pre-season period.

And the pre-season will be strenuous. If you are new to the bike you will first need to establish an aerobic base of about 1,000 miles of steady riding. But once you have that base, the pre-season is the time to develop power. This is the most important single element for the time trialist – you have to have the horsepower to go fast.

About a third of your potential for power is genetically determined: your basic strength, the upper limits of your maximal oxygen uptake and your pain threshold. There is little you can do about these since you can't pick your parents and grandparents. Another third is mental: your willingness to suffer, your desire to win, your ability to concentrate, your motivation. These can be developed with practice. But the final third of the equation is developed with simple sweat from January to March doing specific power-building workouts. These include weight training, ergometer or wind-load simulator, cyclocross riding, hill climbing and big-gear riding. I'll discuss all these power workouts later.

Once you have the power base, you can develop speed starting in April. Power development takes time. If you haven't built the power you need in the pre-season it is too late in June. In contrast, you can improve your speed on short notice if the power base is there.

After you begin regular competition, your goal is to retain the power you have so laboriously developed and peak for certain events so you can ride your best in the most important races. Your weekly schedule will stay very similar to the late pre-season but may include more easy days to compensate for the added stress of competition. You may choose to eliminate the twice-weekly squat routine. And you'll employ specific peaking procedures before big races you especially want to be ready for.

Sample weekly schedules for each period are given on the chart here. Please remember that they are just samples. You will want to modify them to suit your own needs. Most importantly, don't be afraid to take a rest day or an easy day at any time. Some very fine time trialists post phenomenal times on three or four workouts a week, going hard maybe once or twice. Don't overtrain!

Daily principles

Notice that the schedules I have listed give you plenty of room for daily variation. How do you choose what you'll actually do each day when you go out the door? Five principles should guide you as you

SAMPLE WEEKLY TRAINING SCHEDULES	
Preparation period: October, November, December	
Monday	Rest
Tuesday	Weight training and power development on the wind-load simulator
Wednesday	Choose from a 30-mile road ride, an eight-mile run, cross-country skiing or some equivalent aerobic activity
Thursday	One hour of basketball, racquetball or alternate sport
Friday	Weight training and cyclocross or mountain bike riding
Saturday	20-mile road ride, run, WLS, mountain bike ride or equivalent
Sunday	Crosscountry skiing or some other recreational activity
Early pre-season period: January, February	
Monday	Rest
Tuesday	Weights and power workout on the WLS, hill climbing on the road, or power ride on a mountain or cyclocross bike
Wednesday	Conditioning ride on the road or WLS
Thursday	Cyclocross and bike handling drills
Friday	Same as Tuesday
Saturday	Rest, easy skiing, recreation
Sunday	Group ride
Late pre-season period: February, March	
Monday	Light upper-body weight work, rest legs.
Tuesday	Squats, power ride in hills or repeats, etc.
Wednesday	Conditioning ride
Thursday	Intervals, light upper-body weight work
Friday	Easy ride
Saturday	Easy ride or recreational activities
Sunday	Training race or fast group ride preceded by squats

schedule your daily training within this loose framework. They are: know, learn, reason, individualize and choose.

Know means that you understand but only on a superficial level. You know what your training should consist of when you've read everything you can find and talked to other cyclists or listened to your coach. You know when you can say, "Today I've scheduled an easy day and I know that I should pedal easily in 42x19 for one hour because it will promote recovery and get me ready to go hard later."

But mere knowledge is only the first step. The second principle is to *learn*, a word which means a change in behavior. Plenty of cyclists know that a rest day helps them recover or that weight training will make them better riders or that they should do intervals at faster than race pace. But when it comes time to train, they don't put this knowledge into practice. They go through the same standard routines they've always used and wonder why they don't improve.

Their knowledge was useless because they didn't learn from that knowledge — it wasn't accompanied by a meaningful change in behavior. Knowledge is passive, a mere collection of facts. Learning is active; the ability to perceive the facts as living things that can be incorporated into your life to make it different. Knowledge is dead. Learning is alive.

But no matter how much knowledge you gain as a basis for your behavior changes, you need a third component, *reason*. It's the ability to apply your learning to your own situation in a rational, objective way. Reason lets you be skeptical of the advice of others as well as what you think you have learned. The key word here is "why?" Why are you going easy today? Why are you doing intervals? When the group jams hard in training, why are you going with them or dropping off?

Next *individualize*. No training principle is more important than this one. What works well for a world champion like LeMond or Twigg is unlikely to be equally effective for you. And what worked for you last week probably won't work as well now because you are at a different stage of development now than you were then.

The proverb says that you can never step in the same river more than once because the river is always different, always changing, even though to us on the bank it looks the same. Your body's physical rhythms ebb and flow like the river and if you aren't

The first U.S. professional to win a road stage in the Tour de France, Davis Phinney says part of the secret of his success is being able to assimilate a lot of information and put it to use.

aware of that mutability, if you don't go with the flow, you'll be left behind.

Finally, *choice.* Learn what you need and choose it from a large list of possibilities. Need power? Choose from squats, ergometer, hills, cyclocross or repeats depending on the season of the year and your goals. But remember that all training comes down to making the right choices most of the time, day after day, until you reach that goal.

You may think that the fast rider who won today was first because he had a superior cardiovascular system or a lighter bike or more ability to concentrate. Of course these factors are important. But the main reason that rider won while you didn't is because he had made hundreds of training choices in the past year and most of them were correct.

Be a little conservative in your choices. Plan for long-range goals. It is better to take more easy days each week and still be improving in six months than to go hard nearly every day and get injured or stale. Each day ask yourself, "What is the purpose of this workout?" Then choose activities accordingly.

Be aware that choice is a two-edged sword. Whenever we choose, we have to decide, and once we have made a decision we eliminate all other possibilities. If there are five possible workouts that you could do today, they all lie ahead with all their potential intact to help you improve or to make you worse.

But as you consider possibilities and narrow your choices it is like going into a funnel: The act of choosing constricts you to a narrow range of behavior. Decide is a scary word with a frightening end: "cide." That is like suicide, pesticide, herbicide. Successful riders don't decide, they choose from all the options that are available.

The paradox of training

But, you may protest, why can't I just follow the advice of a coach or the specific training schedule in a book and trust to someone else's greater experience? It is true that many top riders follow a coach's instructions to the letter and it may well work if you have a knowledgeable coach who can devote large amounts of time to finding out what you need. Even if you are experienced at self-coaching, as many top riders are, it's good to get a second opinion.

But abdicating complete responsibility for your own improvement to a coach or advisor is a dangerous cop-out for most cyclists. To understand the reason you have to think about the meaning of the word "paradox," a word that will show up frequently in this book. A paradox is a seemingly contradictory statement that, upon closer examination, is not contradictory at all but instead reveals a deeper truth. In fact, there is a strong feeling among some scientists that paradoxes aren't just semantic tricks but are inherent in the real structure of the world – that any deeply profound, important idea can be expressed only in paradoxical terms. The fields of subatomic particles or advanced mathematics (are they really separate fields?) contain many examples.

So what does this excursion into philosophy have to do with time trial training? The central paradox of training is this: You can't believe in training systems but you have to find a system you believe in.

It's easy to fall into the trap of believing that one method of training – intervals, for instance – or one coach's philosophy or one particular weekly schedule will correct all your tactical problems, your deficiencies of power or speed, and help you reach your maximum potential. But assumptions like these are dangerous. You should be as wary of true believers in athletic endeavours as you are in any intellectual arena. The system that worked for some top rider probably won't work for you. A training schedule devised by a famous coach for his national-caliber athletes may destroy you if you are just beginning.

On the other hand, you can't improve if you are skeptical of all systems. You need to develop your own unique blend of workouts – your own system. A workout plan advocated by this year's national champion or one preached fervently by a former Italian pro or one used by your training partner last week may help you improve. Or their systems may leave you floundering from exhaustion or neglecting to work on your weaknesses.

The best system is the one that works for you. The only way to find out what that may be is to try out different systems, objectively decide which one is best, and be ready to modify or discard it completely when it no longer works. Believe – but not blindly.

A problem here is that it is much more difficult to believe in your own system than in one devised by some famous coach or athlete. The name adds authority. We aren't used to trusting ourselves but we have to learn to do it and ignore the intellectual discomfort. Paradoxes are puzzling and distressing at first but reconciling them is a process that has to be gone through by any rider who wants to improve.

Phinney, who has been self-coached for his entire career, advises: "A rider should seek out as many people with knowledge as possible and put together a program that makes the most sense to him or her. Part of the secret of being successful is the ability to assimilate a lot of information and put it to use in the best possible manner for yourself."

5
Weight training
*Legs, arms, back and neck —
cycling demands total body strength*

ONE OF THE MOST important things you can do to improve your time trialing is to train with weights. Of course, basic cycling fitness can only be achieved with long, steady rides. But once that base is established, maximum improvement is possible only if you make strength and power a top training priority.

Why is this true? A strong muscle uses a smaller percentage of its total strength to do a submaximal job. Fewer muscle fibers are recruited, so the muscle doesn't tire as fast. If one cyclist can squat 20 repetitions with 300 pounds and another can manage that many reps with only 200, the first rider uses a much smaller percentage of his total strength when he pedals. He doesn't tire as fast. Of course, he also needs to train on the bike so he can efficiently convert that strength in the squat into several hours of pedaling.

Low repetition, weight-trained strength alone won't suffice. But neither will a steady diet of riding. You need both to approach your potential. As a bonus, when maximum efforts are called for, as in the last leg-searing mile of a time trial or on a hill, you will have more strength to work with. You can build this kind of power with big-gear efforts on hills or into the wind but weight training is a more efficient method.

Leg strength is not all that's required in cycling. You need upper-body strength to stabilize your pedaling motion. Lower-back strength is crucial to time trialing in a big gear. Next time you ride, touch the muscles along your lower spine as you pedal and feel the rhythmic contractions. When you sprint away from the line out of the saddle, notice how you pull on the bars like you are doing a power clean. Cycling demands total body strength but it doesn't stimulate its development. Supplemental strength training is vital.

One striking effect of weight training in any sport is the way it can develop an average athlete into a much better one. Well-trained athletes with natural world-class strength will always dominate. But the general level of competition in all sports has risen dramatically simply because many more athletes are strong and powerful, not just the genetically gifted ones. Think what this means for you, especially when not all cyclists have begun to lift seriously. A winter of strength work could put you ahead of your competitors.

Olavarri says, "Weight training three times a week with Olympic (free) weights is the key to my fall and winter training. I do lots of leg work: full squats, cleans, etc. – power lifting."

Obviously weight training offers many advantages to the cyclist. Now for the bad news. Currently there is no agreement on the best way to develop strength, although several theories are being argued and examined. I'll explain how you might set up a training program using some of these methods. However, the plan you use is less important than the fact that you are lifting. Any well-designed program will produce gains regardless of the hype that emanates from some of the more commercial programs and devices.

A word on specific exercises. First, get an experienced lifter or coach to show you correct form. I'm going to assume that you know the names and can properly perform the exercises I'll mention. Personal help is the only way to be sure you are doing them for maximum benefit. A series of pictures just isn't effective.

Second, free weights are less expensive than machines, are usually more available and, according to many experts, are more effective. So I'll mention several specific exercises that will help your time trialing but can't be done on machines. If you want to use machines, try to find the closest equivalent movement.

Squats

Squats are the basic exercise for time trial power. They develop the all-important quadriceps but they also work your whole power column from knees to lower back. Make sure you do them in good form and use light weights at first or you'll have incredibly sore quads and hamstrings two days later.

I recommend that you squat to a position where your thighs are parallel to the floor but no lower. Full squats have their advocates and it is undoubtedly an advantage to exercise a muscle through a full range of motion. However, they are much more difficult to learn

Weight training can help develop the lower-back strength necessary to push big gears.
Notice Thurlow Rogers' aerodynamic helmet cover and booties for this windy uphill
time trial in the Coors Classic.

to do correctly. For inexperienced lifters the added risk isn't worth
the slight benefit. Also, parallel squats are more specific to cycling
because they duplicate the bend in your knee during the power
phase of the pedal stroke.

I also recommend fairly high repetitions for your squat workout.
This will force you to use lighter weights and decrease the risk of
injury, but there is a more important advantage. Exercise physiologists define power as work over time. Traditional strength tests and
competitions measure gains with a one-repetition maximum lift.
Such strength is of little benefit to a cyclist who has to pedal
thousands of revolutions in a time trial. But power – the ability
to perform many repetitions in a short time – is obviously vital
to time trial success. This being so, 50 reps in the squat is more beneficial than 10 because training should be specific to athletic performance.

It may be argued that, if this is true, why not dispense with squats
and just ride hard in big gears? The answer is that you are building

strength and power along a continuum. You have high resistance, low reps on one end (squats) and low resistance, high reps on the other (easy spinning). You need the whole range of effort in your training.

In the preparation period most riders do two squat workouts a week with 3-6 sets, 10-50 reps each, and moderate weights. One day, for instance (and the weights listed are just examples), a fit rider might do a 50-rep warmup set with 135 pounds, a transitional set of 30 reps with 185, and as many reps as possible with 215 going to exhaustion. If he chose the weight correctly, he will get 30-40 reps on the last set before he succumbs.

This is intense work. To reduce the chances of burning out mentally, on the other day of the week devoted to squats do two sets of 20 with increasing weight (say, 135 and 205) for a warmup. Then do 4-5 sets of 15-20 reps with a weight 10-20% higher than the heaviest you used on high-repetition days. Try to allow as little time as possible between sets, but even that small break is a welcome mental relief. If you try to do 30-50 reps per set to exhaustion twice a week you'll lose your enthusiasm for squats in a hurry.

Other exercises

The second important muscle group that you need to work is the lower back. Squats do some of it. Back extensions are excellent if you have the right equipment. Another possibility is the Good Morning. I like hang cleans with moderate weight. Whatever you choose, start very gradually and never go to maximum since your lower back is susceptible to injury.

Next, do rowing motions to strengthen your arms and upper back. Do a bent row and notice how your position is very similar to your aerodynamic time trial position on the bike. Upright rows are good too and strengthen the trapezius muscles that help support your neck.

Finally, do abdominal and neck-strengthening exercises every time you lift in the pre-season and three times per week the rest of the year. Cycling does nothing for your stomach muscles but if they get weak you may become susceptible to back trouble. I like crunchers which I do while lying on my back with my knees bent and my feet flat on the floor. I hold a 25- to 45-pound plate behind my head and curl my shoulders and upper body up as far as possible. Work up to 75 reps without weight and then add a plate, five pounds at a time. Again, just curl your head and shoulders. Don't do complete sit-ups because they work the wrong muscles and lead to back problems.

Strengthen your neck with wrestler's bridges, a neck harness, neck isometrics, or on a special machine designed to work the neck muscles in all four directions.

Other useful exercises include incline presses, shoulder shrugs, dead lifts, calf raises, leg curls, leg extensions, and lat pull-downs.

Although I think squats are most effectively done using the sets and reps that I just mentioned, there are many ways to organize the other weight training movements into a useful program.

Circuit training

One way to incorporate your chosen exercises into a routine is circuit training. Some experienced weight training coaches dislike it, believing it to be inefficient to try to build both strength and cardiovascular function with weights. However, circuit training is used extensively by cyclists at the Olympic Training Center as well as in Eastern bloc countries. In practice it seems to be a good method of increasing strength and maintaining some aerobic fitness during the preparation period.

Circuit training workouts are convenient regardless of your facilities. They can be done with free weights or on a Universal or similar machine, with calisthenics and body-weight exercises like pull-ups, or with a quick trip through 10 or 12 stations at the local Nautilus center. The only requirement is that 20-second bouts of intense work are separated by equal amounts of rest time. It helps to do your circuit with a training partner. That way he can rest while you do a set and you can encourage each other.

One big advantage of circuit training is the variety possible. If you use your imagination, you can do circuits twice a week for months and never duplicate a workout.

Be careful not to use too much weight. You want to do about 10-15 reps in the 20 seconds and be able to get through the whole sequence without losing form or cheating on the exercise. Remember that your cardiovascular system is getting a workout because of the fast movement from one exercise to the next so the amount of weight you can handle will be limited by your huffing and puffing.

Do most of the movements at a steady controlled rate to help you avoid injury. Pumping even relatively light weights too fast can pull muscles or strain ligaments. Equally important, if you go too fast and throw the weight, most of the work is done by momentum.

Your muscles won't be exercised through the full range of motion. So do each exercise steadily and concentrate on the muscles you are working.

Here is a simple circuit that you can do with only a 110-pound barbell set, a chinning bar, a simple bench, and about 40 square feet of floor area. Weights given are only samples to illustrate how to change the barbell plates quickly. A drawback of doing the circuit with free weights instead of a Universal machine is that it takes longer to alter the weight. However, a little planning will enable you to change the weight in the 20-second rest period. For example:

1. Cleans (75 pounds).

2. Crunchers.

3. Bent-over rowing. (Use the same weight that you used in the clean.)

4. Push-ups. (You can substitute dips if you have a rack.) During the rest period following this exercise, add weight to the bar in preparation for:

5. Squats (110 pounds).

6. Pull-ups. (Vary the grip each time through the circuit: palms away, palms toward you, wide grip, narrow grip, behind the neck.) After the pull-ups, take a 5- and a 2.5-pound plate off each end of the bar.

7. Bench press (95 pounds). Then take 20 pounds off each end.

8. Upright rows (55 pounds).

9. Neck bridges (for the all-important neck muscles). When they get too easy, put a weight on your chest. Pad the floor or wear an old cycling helmet to protect your head. Some people prefer a neck harness, available for $10 from a sporting goods dealer.

10. Jumping squats (75 pounds). Pad the bar with a towel for this one.

Go through the complete circuit once the first time you try it. Eventually you'll want to work up to three times through with two to four minutes of rest between trips.

To make this circuit much more difficult, alternate a 100-yard fast run with each exercise. Or, if you have a wind-load simulator, get on and go hard for 30 seconds. Rope skipping, squat thrusts, and running in place are all possibilities. The idea is to get your heart rate up.

If you don't have access to weights, you can still do a respectable circuit with calisthenics. Aerobic exercise classes at athletic clubs can be excellent circuit workouts too because they are little more than calisthenics to music. Many clubs grade their aerobics sessions according to difficulty so look for the toughest one. You can make any workout of this type more difficult by doing every movement as vigorously as you can and by wearing leg and ankle weights. Nautilus centers, with their emphasis on fast movement from one exercise station to the next, are another way to do circuit training.

One-set theory

Another popular method of weight training for athletes is the one-set-to-exhaustion technique. After a warmup, only one set of each exercise is done but with a weight that allows only 8-12 reps before momentary muscular failure. Proponents of this method argue that if a muscle is worked to exhaustion once, repeated exercises serve no useful purpose since the muscle can't be stimulated to further improvement until it recovers and is exhausted again two days later.

According to this theory, multiple sets are a waste of time and energy. If you go all-out on one set, you've produced all the improvement you can for that workout. (The theory behind Nautilus is similar.) This approach is controversial but has advantages for the time trialist with limited training time who has to be out putting in some miles and can't be spending hours in the weight room.

If you use this technique, be sure to do each repetition slowly and strictly. Concentrate on the muscles you are working. Don't cheat by arching your back in the bench press or assisting in the upright row with your legs. Ideally you should have a training partner who can spot for you. When you can't do another rep by yourself, say after nine, he can help you force out another three reps so you work the muscle to the maximum.

A drawback of the one-set method is the danger of mental fatigue. It's tough to push to exhaustion and you can get thoroughly sick of the whole procedure. Another is the idea of exercising to failure. Who wants to fail? Yet when you train this way you fail on every exercise every day you lift. This seems to violate the "train for success" maxim. However, you have to accept the paradox inherent in weight training. Only by failing to make that last repetition do you force the muscle to grow stronger. When you lift, failure is success.

For the time trialist, the following is a sample one-set workout using free weights, to be done during the preparation period.

1. Bench press
2. Bent-over rowing or corner rows

National team members work with weights year-round, as at this early season training camp in Texas.

3. Weighted dips
4. Weighted pull-ups
5. Crunchers with weights
6. Back extensions
7. Leg extensions
8. Leg curls
9. Squats
10. Neck bridges

Remember, don't do lower back or neck exercises to failure because of the risk of injury.

I do this routine fairly frequently but I do two sets of most exercises. The first is a warmup set using lighter weights and submaximum reps. Then I add weight and go to exhaustion on the second set. Many authorities tell you that a warmup set is a waste of time because the warmup that takes place during the first five or six reps of a set is sufficient. This hasn't been my experience. And quite a few people seem to get injured when they do one set to maximum without a formal warmup of the specific muscles involved.

Of course you don't have to do any of the exercises to failure in order to get some benefit from them. However, the more thoroughly you exhaust the muscle, the more improvement you'll create as long as you allow sufficient rest between exercise bouts.

This method of weight training is especially useful during the season if you restrict it to the upper body. It is quick, so you can do it in 15 minutes before or after a ride and one set is not so exhausting that you have no energy left over to train. Yet you can increase muscle strength, even at the height of the racing season, instead of just maintaining it.

Putting it all together

Here is a general year-round weight training plan for the time trialist. It is based on the theory of periodization that I described in an earlier chapter. Be sure to vary the workouts within each segment. Don't do the same squat routine six weeks in a row, for example.

October 1 to November 15: Do a general program for the whole body. Use fairly light weights, 1-3 sets, a wide variety of exercises, and don't go to maximum. Keep the physical and mental stress moderate because the purpose is to work all the muscles and prepare them for more intensive work later.

November 15 to January 1: Circuit training. In most climates it is hard to ride much during this period because of darkness, bad weather, or both. Vigorous circuit training takes up some of the aerobic slack caused by time off the bike and it is more strenuous than the light training that you did in October.

January 1 to February 15: Power phase for the legs. Start building your power with 3-5 sets of squats using 15-30 repetitions. It's preferable to do the squat workout only twice a week on Tuesday or Thursday and again on Sunday, days when you are also doing hard riding on the wind-load simulator or on the road. This gives your legs plenty of time to recover from the hard days. If you work them hard with squats one day and ride hard the next, recovery time is too short. The idea is to really blitz the legs with squats and power work on the bike all in one day, then let them recover fully before you do it again.

Alternate upper-body workouts with squats, usually doing them on Monday and Friday, days when you'll be taking it easy after hard riding days. Increase upper-body strength using the one-set-to-exhaustion method to save time and energy needed for the legs to adapt.

February 15 to April 1: Retain the one-set upper body workouts on Monday and Friday and squats on Tuesday and Sunday. Change the squat workout to 3-5 sets of up to 50 reps with lighter weights to increase your power.

April 1 to October 1: Light upper-body workouts twice a week on days when you ride easily. Leg work in the form of squats is optional depending on whether your experience has shown that it helps you get stronger or makes you tired. In any case, discontinue weight work for the legs at least two weeks before major events that you want to be at your best for.

6
Winter riding

Outdoors or in, here's a way to put
some variety into your off-season

DURING THE preparation and early pre-season periods I recommend several alternate kinds of riding. If the weather is bad you may want to work out on an indoor trainer. And for variety − both mental and physical − try mountain bikes or cyclocross. But what equipment do you need for these activities and what kind of workout should you do? Here are some guidelines.

Wind-load simulators

For years the only indoor cycling devices readily available were rollers and ergometers. Rollers were fine for working on spin or sweating a gallon, but most of them didn't produce enough resistance for muscular training. Ergometers were expensive and the upright bars, mattress saddles and rattrap pedals made it impossible for most riders to duplicate their road position.

Now all that has changed. Sophisticated rollers, like the Kreitler system, have fans to increase resistance. Ergometers are more readily available in bike shops and catalogs. Some, like the Tunturi, come with dropped bars, racing saddles, toeclips, and a widely adjustable fore-and-aft saddle position.

The biggest change has been the introduction of wind-load simulators (WLS). These clever devices, originally marketed by Racer-Mate but widely copied since, have all sorts of advantages over any other system. They allow you to use your own bike so your position is not changed. They are fairly inexpensive, running from $100 for a basic but perfectly serviceable model up to $300 for one with covered fans and speedometer. They all feature attachment systems that let you use nearly any bike, including those with cable guides under the bottom bracket. Most allow you to switch bikes on the same stand in seconds, an advantage for clubs or when several riders use the same one.

But the major advantage of the WLS is that the little squirrel-cage fans produce more and more resistance the faster you pedal and the bigger gear you use. The rap against rollers is that for a fit cyclist they aren't hard enough, but that can't be said of the WLS. In a moderate gear at a brisk cadence you can get a great workout. And in a 53x12 you can hurt yourself severely.

In fact, a powerhouse rider like Potoff, who is more than capable of hammering big gears in his road training, believes that for indoor training "too much resistance is counterproductive. I prefer to ride a fixed-gear track bike on a set of moderately light resistance rollers. It gives me the opportunity to loosen up and generate more leg speed than I normally employ while training or racing."

Keep in mind that Potoff lives in Arizona and can get out on the road all winter for some high-resistance work. Riders who live in snowy climates need to do some power development and for that a WLS is ideal. A great setup is to have rollers for spinning on days when you want to go easy and a WLS for harder days. Or you can ride rollers with an original Racer-Mate attached to the seatpost for more resistance than on rollers alone.

Setting up the space

Since you won't be outside on the road surrounded by the diversions of weather, traffic, and other cyclists, it pays to arrange the indoor environment around your WLS.

If you have the space, set up a separate workout room. A spare bedroom is good or a corner of the basement, preferably with a window you can look out while riding. Even an unheated garage works since you'll generate plenty of warmth — enough to heat the garage and probably the room above it. Some riders use apartment balconies.

I have commandeered half of our downstairs family room. It has a built-in desk in one corner with a pegboard behind it where I hang bike parts. My spare wheels hang above it. I built a makeshift squat rack into one wall with my weights stored below. The floor is carpeted so I put the WLS on a 4x4 sheet of plywood to provide a more stable base and keep my sweat from falling on the carpet. The WLS is directly in front of a window so I get all the ventilation I need without a fan, but you should consider one if you don't have a convenient window. The fans on the WLS provide quite a bit of resis-

The fans on a wind-load simulator produce more resistance the faster you pedal, and the attachment system can be adapted to almost any bike.

tance but their cooling properties are overrated. The desk is next to the WLS so I keep a tape deck and a selection of cassettes there. The headphone cord reaches conveniently also.

Before you start to ride, get out plenty of cassettes, a bottle of water and maybe some sort of energy replacement drink – you'll need it. Drape a spare T-shirt and headband over a nearby chair since the clothes you start in will be soaked long before the session is over. Scrounge up several old but still absorbent towels. Put one within reach to wipe sweat off your face since the thirstiest headband will be saturated quickly. Wrap another towel around the headset and stem, securing it with a clothespin, to keep your sweat from corroding the recessed stem bolt or seeping down into the head tube. (A light coat of WD-40 on both the bike and the frame of the WLS helps too.) Spread out another towel on the floor below you over the main rail of your WLS to soak up the rivers of sweat that will cascade onto the carpet. Without a towel you'll soon be pedaling in a puddle.

WLS workouts

I think that the most effective use of the WLS during the winter is to build power. It provides enough resistance to stress even the strongest rider if you use big gears. What kind of workouts will do this? Eddie B recommends the following as the best drill for power. Warm up for 15 to 20 minutes in low to medium gears. Then do three consecutive periods of three minutes each in progressively higher gears at a cadence of 90. Your heart rate should be 175-185 (depending on your age) during the last minute of the last set. Cool down in a low gear for 10 minutes and repeat.

The gears you use and the number of repetitions will depend on your fitness and the time of year. For instance, if you are a seasoned rider in good shape who wants a strenuous workout, you might warm up for 5-10 minutes in a 42x19 and then a 42x17. Follow that with three minutes in 53x19, three minutes in 53x17, and finish with the last three in 53x15, never letting your cadence drop below 90. Use a bike computer to monitor your cadence or check it frequently by counting for 15 seconds and multiplying by four. Pedal easily in 42x17 for 10 minutes and do it all over again. A 10-minute cooldown and you're done: a hard workout in 50-60 minutes maximum.

As your power improves, increase the gearing. In the hypothetical example I gave, you'd go to 53x18, 16, and 15. Or increase resistance in one-tooth intervals: 53x17, 16, 15.

Remember that these figures are just examples. Use what you can handle on your unit since the resistance of different machines varies and so does the resistance of different tire combinations. Incidentally, I have had bad luck using tubular tires on a WLS. The tread bubbled up and the casing ruptured after only a ride or two. Many cyclists seem to have no trouble but now I use high-pressure clinchers.

Eddie suggests that time trialists do these workouts once a week from December 1 to January 15 and then twice weekly until February 15. They also substitute effectively for hard road rides later in the season if the weather is bad.

A word of warning. It isn't advisable to get out of the saddle forcefully to keep your gear rolling at the end of a repeat or to do sprints. Most WLS stands aren't stable enough or designed for it. If you topple over you could hit your head on something or bend the front dropouts on your bike where they attach to the stand. It is embarrassing to crash when you aren't moving, too.

This sort of tough winter training will build your power but it has another equally important function. As Deborah Shumway observes: "These workouts help me deal with mental pain and stress which are so necessary for effective time trialing."

You can also do on the WLS any of the interval or repeat workouts that you would normally do on the road later in the season. But don't overdo it. It is tempting to start doing hard repeats in December thinking that you'll be that much ahead of the competition in April. A more likely result is that you'll get tired and stale by April, ride badly, and take up fishing or chess by July when the big events are held.

You can use the WLS for longer conditioning rides too but I find that more than an hour at a steady pace gets boring. And you can fall victim to the dread "numb crotch syndrome" if you don't move around on the saddle. But sometimes there's no choice.

I like to get out on the road at least once a week even in the coldest Colorado January for a reasonably long ride to burn some calories and avoid cabin fever. When it is too snowy the solution is obvious but painful: I spend an equivalent amount of time on a WLS.

There are some solutions to the boredom problem. Don't try to do a two-hour session in the same moderate gear even on long steady rides or you'll succumb to blind despair. Vary the effort a little without going too hard. If you have a vivid imagination, visualize your favorite training route and ride it in your head, simulating the hills by shifting to a bigger gear and spinning downhill in a lower one.

A bike computer provides an instant, visual feedback of your effort. This is invaluable since the usual indicators of speed like the feel of the wind, road vibration, or roadside trees rushing past are all absent. WLS stands require removal of the front wheel that the speed and distance function of most bike computers depend on. So invest in a rear-wheel mounting unit and you'll be able to monitor your cadence as well as do actual time trials where you can see exactly how long it takes to roll over 10 miles on the read-out. The result shouldn't be taken as an indication of your actual 10-mile time on the road since the resistance of the units varies so much, but the time is still a great comparative device from one month of workouts to another.

Off-road riding done to stay in shape and improve bike handling skills paid off in a national cyclocross title for Roy Knickman.

Mountain bikes and cyclocross

It is a popular winter cycling event in Europe that is rapidly catching on here. Eddie B recommends it for winter training and riders at the Olympic Training Camp do it several times a week in the off-season. It will build your time trial power, help you retain your aerobic fitness over the winter, and make you a bombproof bike handler able to leap logs and potholes in a single bound. And it may be the best kept secret in the arsenal of top riders' training techniques. What it is it? Off-road riding on cyclocross bikes or their American cousins, mountain bikes.

It doesn't seem to make much difference if you do off-road riding on a road bike modified for cyclocross with knobby tires and low gears or on a mountain bike. Nor do you need to look for cyclocross competition and practice the sport's specialized skills like dismounting, clearing obstacles and remounting. Informal off-road training is all that is necessary.

Why should you ride in the dirt, snow and mud or work on bike handling skills if you are mainly interested in time trials? Regardless of your event, you need to be the best bike handler possible within the genetic limitations of your eye-hand coordination, balance, and kinesthetic sense. One reason this is so is because you will probably want to train with other riders even if you prefer to limit your competition to individual time trials. Fast group training with better riders is one of the best ways to increase your ability.

Group rides are sometimes more dangerous than races because the riders may be more inattentive or fatigued. Also, training groups are usually mixed, with experienced steady riders next to erratic novices. So if your bike handling skills aren't honed, the danger of crashes may outweigh the considerable physiological value of group rides. Even if you are willing to take the chance, you may not be welcome if you aren't a good bike handler.

In the unlikely event that you always train alone, you need bike handling skills to protect you from potholes, graveled corners, oil slicks, snarling dogs and your own inattention. And you are never really alone since cars are far more dangerous than the most squirrelly fellow rider. If you can't ride a straight line, overtaking vehicles may clip you. Riding down a traffic-choked street requires the same pack riding skills as mass-start racing with more severe penalties for a mistake. For all these reasons, you owe it to yourself to become comfortable on the bike in any situation and off-road riding will improve your skills fast.

It may seem slow, but winter mountain bike riding can help build the power that translates into more speed in the spring.

Doing it in the dirt also expands your training terrain. Where I live in western Colorado quite a few of the roads are dirt or gravel. On my road bike I am restricted to three or four basic routes with minor variations. On a mountain bike there is no real limit at all. Places to ride are everywhere. In cities, try jogging paths around the perimeters of parks or ride around large playing fields or undeveloped land. In more rural settings head for irrigation ditch roads, fire roads, farmer's tractor trails around fields, or gravel roads in the country.

For a time trialist another important by-product of mountain bike riding is that it builds power which translates into more speed on your road bike come spring. Grewal, a top climber and stage racer, says that he builds power by climbing steep gravel hills near his home in Aspen. No hills? No problem. If you live in the flatlands, powering through loose dirt or six inches of heavy snow will give your quads a workout and accustom you to big gears on your road bike.

During the off-season, devote one day a week to bike handling drills. Set up a course that's about a half mile around in a field or park. Put in as many corners as possible that take advantage of the natural contours. For instance, locate sharp corners around trees or at the bottom of hills. It is just as useful to ride around an area free-lancing as the mood hits. In either case, include some 180-degree turns to simulate the turnaround in a time trial and do 5 or 10 of these each session. Such practice will guard against the chance of inadvertently increasing your time by the number of seconds or minutes required to get back up after crashing at the turnaround cone. Practice your starts too, powering off the line as if it were a road time trial.

What kind of bike?

Should you use a cyclocross bike or invest in a mountain bike? Quite a few riders are now using mountain bikes for off-season riding and training. Others are hesitant because they are afraid that the upright position on the bike will develop the wrong muscles and reflexes for time trialing. However, if the saddle position on the mountain bike is similar to that on your road bike, the upright handlebars won't cause any problem. Sure, your position will be different but this may even be an advantage because you'll work your muscles in different ways during the winter. There is plenty of time to re-establish your normal position when you get back on the roads come spring.

If the flat bars are uncomfortable you can convert the mountain bike to dropped bars with little sacrifice of handling or stability on rough ground. It does take a little time and money to do this, and you should first consider the kind of terrain you will be riding. Steep rocky jeep trails or forest paths usually require the added stability of upright bars. If you ride on gravel roads and flatter terrain, consider drops.

Of course you don't need a $500 to $1,000 mountain bike to get all the power benefits of gravel road rides or the bike handling practice of informal cyclocross sessions. A regular road frame with a few modifications will do. I don't advise that you use your good bike, however. The bike you ride in the dirt is going to take its lumps. It will get muddy, wet and scratched. You are likely to ding up the tubes when you crash. A winter spent sliding around in muddy ruts will probably throw the frame out of alignment. It just isn't worth it to subject a $500 frame to needless punishment. It will get plenty in normal training.

Instead of risking your best bike, shop around for a used frame and cheap components and build up a bike that will double for use off-road as well as in winter slop. A used racing frame will do, but something with slightly slacker angles like an old touring frame will be better on rough ground and have more clearance for wider tires and mud build-up. If you live in hilly country equip it with a triple crankset so you can use the two larger chainrings for regular winter road riding and go to the small one on mountain bike terrain. Clincher wheels are cheap, plenty strong, and allow you to use the Tri Cross tires by Specialized if most of your riding will be on dirt or snow. If not, heavy 1¼-inch clinchers with a coarse tread pattern will cut down on punctures and give you some traction on loose surfaces.

Regardless of whether you buy a mountain bike, use a bike designed for cyclocross competition, or resurrect the junker stashed away in your garage, riding off the road in winter will make you a better time trialist when you get back on the road next spring.

7
Wind and weather

*It's best to brave the elements,
but dress for the occasion*

SHOULD YOU train on the road when it's cold, wet, icy, or windy?
And, if so, how can you protect yourself from the elements and even
use them to your benefit?

Many determined time trialists accumulate a substantial base of
road miles during the winter in conditions that would discourage
a non-cyclist from going out in a car. Still, there are some conditions
in which it is preferable not to ride. One is extreme cold, or moderate cold coupled with a strong wind.

It is possible to ride in temperatures that only a penguin could
love but it is questionable whether you get much benefit out of rides
in conditions much below freezing where you are in danger of frostbite on exposed skin like your face. Even unexposed flesh can get
pretty chilly and males are in danger of penile frostbite, a gruesome
price to pay for a few midwinter miles on the bike.

Cold limits your training severely too. For one thing, when it's
cold you should ride only on flat or rolling terrain. Long climbs are
fine because you aren't going very fast uphill so you avoid most of
the windchill and the effort warms you up. But what goes up has
to come down. When you are sweaty from the climb, a four-mile descent at 40 or 50 m.p.h. can be brutal.

A few miles east of town I have two great climbs, one a steady four
miles and the other a steeper six. I've tried to ride these on cold winter days when the pavement was clear but neither a whole Sunday
edition of the local newspaper against my chest nor a minor fortune
in windbreakers, wool Dachstein mitts, polypropylene underwear,
and shoe covers could keep me from being freeze-dried at the bottom
of the hill. Your winter power development is better done in a warm

weight room, sweating over a wind-load simulator, or plowing slowly through snow on a mountain bike.

Even flat rides at fairly reasonable temperatures have their dangers. Wind is the biggest. Ride into it on the outward leg of your training so it will be at your back on the return trip. This cuts down on the windchill factor, especially when you are wet with perspiration, and the tailwind blows you home to that hot shower faster.

Quite a bit has been made of the danger of frosting your lungs because of hard breathing in frigid temperatures. This danger has been ruled out by some exercise physiologists who contend that any air that reaches your lungs has been warmed sufficiently by your throat and nasal passages to eliminate danger. This sounds reasonable – at least I've never had any trouble in the cold, dry air of Colorado and plenty of nordic skiers breathe awfully hard in temperatures below zero with no ill effects. But some riders have persistent bronchial problems. Dan Harding, a local rider and competitive crosscountry skier, uses a face mask to warm the air on cold rides.

Another oft-cited danger from cold is to the ligaments and tendons of the knees. The warmest wool tights are loosely woven and your legs can get chilled no matter how you bundle them up. The newer tights with a nylon windbreak panel sewn in front help cut down windchill substantially but they are expensive.

I haven't had any knee injuries from the cold, even though I wear only one pair of standard wool tights in the coldest conditions. Other riders, however, seem to have a yearly siege of knee problems even if they squeeze into three layers of leg warmers, wool tights, and wind pants. I suspect that either individual tolerance varies widely or those susceptible riders are getting injured for some reasons unrelated to temperature. Perhaps they changed to a different pair of shoes with different cleat adjustments or rode a winter bike that wasn't set up quite the same way as their regular one. (Don't forget, when you wear more layers between yourself and your saddle you will need to lower your seat to keep the same riding position.)

Jack Panek is a rider who lives in Gunnison, Colorado, a town which consistently vies for the dubious distinction of coldest spot in the nation. If you are going to have cold knees anywhere on earth it will probably happen there. Jack says that the best remedy for cold knees is a pair of wrestler's knee pads that he buys for about $5 at the local sporting goods store. He slips them on under layers

One of the best reasons to train in bad weather is because you may have to race in it. Believe it or not, this scene is from the Tour of Italy held in May. That's Italian super-star Francesco Moser in the center. Recent technical innovations in fabrics have made training and racing more bearable in cold and wet weather.

of leg warmers and tights and their thick foam padding keeps even the frigid blasts of Gunnison's main street away from tender tendons. Futhermore, he assures me that they won't bind when you pedal or slip down during a ride. As a bonus, if you crash on the ice, they protect your knees. Be sure they are big enough so they don't constrict your knee tendons or they could cause irritation and tendinitis.

Another situation that precludes serious road riding is streets icy or slippery with snow. You can go out on a mountain bike or cyclocross bike in such conditions and have a great time but a road bike on the streets just isn't safe. You have less control, and the potential damage from crashing – minimal on a cyclocross bike – is magnified by higher speeds. I have a friend who uses regular knobby tires on his mountain bike but modifies them by putting screws through the knobbies so he ends up with a pair of studded snow tires. He reports that they work great for riding on snow-packed or icy roads.

Finally, darkness. It is possible to ride at night, especially around street-lit suburban loops on a well-lighted and reflectorized bike. I used to do it occasionally but now I find the game not worth the candle. It is just too dangerous under most circumstances.

So in darkness, icy streets, and bitter cold, hang up your road bike and either bash around on your clunker or get a great workout at home on an ergometer or training stand.

The cold-weather outfit

All this having been said, I find that I usually prefer outdoor rides in reasonable cold to riding an indoor trainer. There is really no substitute for road riding. Franz Hammer points out that "East German and Polish riders in particular are known to ride in the winter months in often dismal conditions and their success is evident."

If I can keep my hands, ears, and feet warm, I can ride in just about any temperature. For comfortable hands some riders use down mitts which I find too bulky, too expensive, and too intolerant of dampness from sweat. Polypropylene liners with Gore-Tex or a similar overmitt is another common choice but Gore-Tex is so expensive that the thought of wiping off a tire and having that abrasive tread eat into my investment leaves me, if you'll pardon the expression, cold. For the last several winters I've used leather work gloves lined with fleece and found them adequate in most conditions. If it is really bad I layer nylon and leather mitts over them.

Ears are easy. Since a large percent of your body heat is lost through your head, keep it warm. A hardshell helmet with the vent holes taped over works well. Take the sizing pads out of a Bell Tourlite, an MSR, or something similar and there is room for a wool hat underneath. I use just a skier's earband and find that it is plenty. Some helmets have a nylon shell, but the coated material won't let perspiration out and I usually feel like I've been swimming no matter how cold the day.

Feet are tougher to keep warm. The best solution is to get another pair of shoes like your regular ones but a size larger so you can wear thick wool socks. Be sure the cleats are adjusted exactly like your normal shoes. Then get insulated overboots and a pair of those clever little nylon toeclip covers to further reduce windchill. Short of electric socks, that's about all you can do.

I finish off the cold-weather outfit with wool tights, a polypropylene long-sleeved T-shirt, a sleeveless wool T-shirt and a wool cycling jacket with nylon panels on the front and shoulders. That keeps me warm in temperatures above about 20 degrees Fahrenheit. Below that I can't keep my feet warm no matter what I do, so all the clothes in the closet won't help.

Riding in the rain

Some conditions are pretty frightful when you look out at them from the protection of the house. However, they are generally not only possible to ride in but necessary if you are going to develop bike handling skills, mental toughness, and experience in all conditions.

Rain is one. Don't be afraid to ride in the rain. Only by riding on slick streets will you be able to learn how your bike handles in the wet. You don't want to lose valuable seconds by having to get up from a crash at the turnaround of your next rainy time trial. Prepare for wet training rides by wearing waterproof but breathable shells, shoe covers, and a cycling hat with a bill under your helmet to keep the rain out of your eyes.

All those garments catch too much wind to use in competition, though. For rainy races or fast training in reasonably moderate temperatures, most experienced riders use Lycra-type clothing because it doesn't soak up much water. For colder temperatures put a plastic garbage bag with cut-out arms and neck holes under your jersey.

Many racers compete in the cold and wet without long tights. Instead they coat their legs with a warming rub like Cramergesic or one of the mixtures imported from Europe. It has long been an article of faith in cycling that a thick coat of grease will protect your knees from the cold better than any fabric covering. Riders argue that even Lycra is useless when it gets wet. And some view wearing tights in a race as an admission that you lack toughness.

I feel that with form-fitting Lycra clothing you will be just as fast wearing long tights as without. To be on the safe side you can use a liberal coating of Cramergesic, or a similar heating rub, plus the tights and let those self-proclaimed tough riders scowl in derision. It is a small price to pay compared to six weeks off the bike with tendinitis. And that goes double in training.

Use the wind

Severe wind is more a psychological deterrent than a physical danger unless it reaches hurricane force. Most windy days are merely unpleasant, especially when dust and dirt are blowing in your eyes.

Wind, however, is one of those disadvantages that can be turned into a plus. View a windy day as an opportunity to work on your power and aerodynamic position in the headwind parts. Then work on your leg speed when the gales are at your back. You are going to have to deal with wind in your racing and the best place to learn how is in training when the flags whip loudly, stoplights sway above intersections, and billboards creak and groan.

I once heard Colorado Springs called a great place to train because it's windy and hilly. Florida, California, the desert southwest, or the flat lands of the midwest all have their share of wind too. What is unpleasant for casual riding is superb for the sort of hard work that makes you stronger, faster, and mentally tough.

What if you have an easy day scheduled and you wake to gale-force winds? One alternative is to ride a short circuit, say four miles around, so you get the gale only for short periods of time. Use a very low gear to fulfill the easy-day requirement of little or no pressure on the pedals. Here in western Colorado we get some spring days when it seems that most of Utah is about to be blown across state lines and I've found a 42x24 on the flat to be about right. The tailwind section in a 53x12 is easy spinning too.

Another alternative is to choose roads sheltered from the wind by trees, hedgerows, tall cornfields, or big buildings. But one of the problems with windy plains regions like Colorado is that the lack of vegetation means that nearly all roads are unprotected. The Colorado district championship time trial course is east of Denver and should be ideal for record attempts. It's at altitude, flat, and straight. In fact, Sain set the then-national record on the course in 1978. The catch is that a fairly calm day is a rarity on the high plains. It isn't uncommon to ride from the start propelled by 30 m.p.h. winds, then grind back in teeth-clenched misery. One year, when the day of the championship was windy, riders went as much as seven minutes slower than their best times on a calm day.

8

Pre-season conditioning rides

*Steady miles build endurance
that will last you all season*

LET'S ASSUME you've worked hard all winter in the weight room
and on the wind-load simulator. You've skidded around in the mud
or snow doing cyclocross. Now it's time to get in some road miles.
However, you can't just jump on the bike and ride it at midseason
levels even if you've been grinding away winter's gloom on a WLS.
There's no way to duplicate the demands of actual riding on an indoor trainer, so re-establishing your base with steady riding on the
road is priority number one in the pre-season.

Although most riders think of leg-searing solo intervals or competitive group rides when they think of training, much of the everyday riding of even top racers consists of less intense, steady efforts.

Steady rides, done three or four days a week, serve different training functions. In the preparation period and early pre-season they
help you establish a base of fitness. Then, as the season progresses,
they are used to build endurance. During the competition period
steady rides are important for recovery.

Your aerobic base

The usual term for the kind of steady riding which is done to gain
fitness is LSD. This was originally an acronym for "long slow distance" but most riders now change the "slow" to "steady." Long slow
rides, when you twiddle along stopping every hour for a picnic, are
fun for some people and a great way to see scenic country but they
don't do much for fitness except in the most basic way.

I prefer to drop the LSD designation since it is misleading and smacks of the drug culture. I substitute the term "conditioning ride" instead. It is less catchy but not as unsavory and more accurate. The time trialist needs two distinct kinds of these conditioning rides during the course of the year.

The first is done in the pre-season when you initially get back on your bike. You should ride spinning easily in low gears at a cadence of 90-100 r.p.m. Increase the distance as you regain your road fitness after a winter of weight training, alternate sports and WLS work. If you are just getting started on the bike, these rides will establish your aerobic base.

The emphasis here is on establishing a good foundation of aerobic fitness as well as getting your ligaments and tendons used to the pedaling motion again. If you have spent the winter running, skiing or in some other off-bike activity this period of easy riding is necessary to avoid injury when you start to push harder.

On the other hand, if you live where you can ride most of the year and cycling is your preferred means of fitness you've probably been doing some rides like this all winter. This is benchmark training that you can do day after day for basic fitness any time of the year. And if your interest is long time trials, point-to-point record attempts, or the transcontinental race this sort of riding will constitute most of your training.

Conditioning for endurance

The second type of conditioning ride begins when you have a good base of about 1,000 miles of easy to moderate spinning. At this point your rides begin to get longer, faster, and you use a bigger gear as you gain fitness. These rides are normally done on Wednesday. During the early season when you are trying to build endurance and stamina you'd probably ride 40-50 miles in a 63- to 70-inch gear at about 18-20 m.p.h. if you are a one-hour 40km time trialist. Finish pleasantly tired but not wiped out.

Be conservative. Runners have found that they should train perhaps five out of seven days at a pace at least a minute per mile slower that their 10-kilometer race pace. This gives them recovery. Then two days a week they either race or do speedwork at a faster-than-race pace.

This idea can be converted to cycling. Suppose a runner races at six minutes per mile. His usual training pace for steady runs would be seven minutes per mile, or 16% slower. In the same way, if you time trial at 25 m.p.h. your training pace on Wednesday's solo con-

Long steady rides establish your fitness base in the early season and help build endurance. Later in the year, easy rides are done for rest and recovery.

ditioning ride should be about 20 m.p.h. You'll get your chance to go faster on Tuesday and Thursday.

This second type of ride shouldn't be done too close to your anaerobic threshold regardless of what the watch says. Anaerobic threshold is a physiologist's term that means the rate of exertion where a little more output would put you into oxygen debt. When you time trial all-out for 25 miles you are pushing at the edge of the anaerobic threshold. When you jam to go over a little hill and begin to gasp and pant for air, you're over the edge – you've gone into oxygen debt and you have to ease up on the downhill to recover.

If you did your conditioning rides at the anaerobic threshold they would become too mentally demanding and the physical recovery would take too long to enable you to do faster work the next day. Conditioning rides should be done at a brisk, steady pace.

Training heart rate

How can you tell what is the right pace for your conditioning rides? A standard answer is to go at a tempo which makes your heart beat at 75-85% of its maximum. You can check your heart rate while riding by feeling the big carotid artery in your neck next to your windpipe. Use one hand while you keep the other on the bars. Count the pulse for 15 seconds and multiply by four.

The usual formula for your theoretical maximum heart rate is to subtract your age from 220. Then take 75-85% of that figure to find the heart rate that you should strive for in a conditioning ride. A 30-year-old would subtract 30 from 220 to get a maximum heart rate of 190. 75% of that is 142 and 85% is 161 so this rider should aim for a heart rate of 142-161 on long rides. This method certainly isn't foolproof but it is interesting to check yourself occasionally.

The "220 minus your age" figure is just a statistical average so you may want to find out exactly what your maximum heart rate is and work from there. A few years ago I took the infamous ergometer test at the Olympic Training Center in Colorado Springs. It involves pedaling a steady cadence on increasing resistance until exhaustion. Heart rate is monitored. At age 37, my projected maximum heart rate was 183 but my poor heart got up to 193 before my legs and my desire both collapsed simultaneously. I had suspected that, since I don't feel like I am getting much out of a workout unless my heart rate is 8-10 beats per minute faster than the figures derived in the traditional way.

After you take your pulse a few times while riding you will develop a sense of what the correct range feels like so you won't have to fumble around trying to find that artery every five minutes. Very few experienced cyclists monitor their heart rates. Instead they listen to their bodies. As running guru Dr. George Sheehan writes: "Pulse rates are for scientists and their studies. Do not let their science interfere with your practice."

You can, of course, check your heart rate with one of the electronic monitors available from cycling and running suppliers. The heart rate band on the Pacer 2000 from Veltec is a good example. Some of these units are fairly accurate while others flash you a number on the monitor that seems to have absolutely no relationship to what you are doing at the moment. I dislike the technical gimmickry, not to mention the expense, of such devices and have been perfectly happy to check my pulse, on the rare occasions when I do it, with my hand and a watch.

If you use a heart rate monitor, don't forget to watch the road ahead. One rider I know was so mesmerized by the numbers that he ran into the back of a parked car. He trashed his bike, put a big dent in his helmet, and bruised his knee badly. He was profoundly embarrassed at the incident. However the little electronic gadget kept on flashing after the impact, still hanging tenaciously to the bars of his twisted bike, and the rider couldn't help noting his heart rate as they carted him off to the hospital. If you are that hung up on bio-feedback, maybe you can't get along without one.

Gearing and distance

Be careful on longer conditioning rides not to overgear. Overgearing can strain your knees and it also fosters a square, labored pedal stroke. There is no reason to practice bad habits for two or three hours.

On the other hand, some riders believe that using a slightly larger gear on these rides helps their power. Resh says, "I use big gears in training – 53x17 at least on the flats – to give me the strength to ride a good time trial." Remember that he rode a 56:08 to place sixth in the 1983 nationals so compare your results to his and reduce your training gears proportionally. Regardless of your gear choice, keep your cadence above 90 and concentrate on a smooth and supple pedal action.

How long should your weekly conditioning ride be? It depends on the length of the time trials that you are aiming for. If you compete at 25 miles, 40-60 miles on a training ride is probably enough. If you go shorter on your conditioning rides, you won't burn much fat nor will your body be stimulated enough to begin to develop the capillary system that transports oxygen to the working muscles. Much longer and you won't be going fast enough to improve.

What about longer rides? Many time trialists like to ride 10- to 25-mile time trials, but on the weekends they don't race they like to go 100 miles or more, sometimes pretty fast. These rides are great therapy and they burn a lot of fat. They can be too slow to give you much direct benefit but they produce a great base. The exception is if you do them in a fast group at 25 m.p.h. or so. Then the ride is like four hours of motorpacing and will build stamina and speed that translates directly into fast time trials.

Of course if you go in for long time trials like 12- or 24-hour events or point-to-point record rides, long rides will be the cornerstone of your training. And you'll probably have to do them several times a week at the expense of faster training.

Finally, don't be afraid of long climbs if you have some mountains in your area. "What helps my strength the most," says Kiefel, "is riding three to five hours in the mountains, steady." And his teammate Phinney agrees: "I like to take mountain rides once a week to develop big gear strength." Casebeer adds, "I find that when I train on the flats I lose a lot of strength that I get from hills. But too much climbing makes you strong but slow."

But don't worry about losing speed when you are cranking out the miles, vertical or horizontal, on conditioning rides. You need that base of power and aerobic fitness before you can get fast. And speed is the subject of the next chapter.

Easy Rides

There is another type of steady ride which is slower and shorter than the conditioning rides I have been discussing. Called easy rides, they punctuate your harder training or racing so they are done primarily for recovery. And they should be easy: slow, with little mental involvement in the actual riding. Think about keeping your pedal cadence around 90 but forget other concerns, like riding form, that you concentrate on during your speedwork days. Cruise along and look at the scenery.

Choose a flat road so you don't have to work to climb hills. Eddie B advises that on easy days you use a gear so low that you don't feel any resistance at all when you pedal. Even for strong riders this means 42x18 to 42x20 on the flat. Take it easy, relax and spin your legs. If you feel good and are tempted to go faster or if you feel guilty that you aren't, just think about how rested and eager you will be to go hard tomorrow.

Easy rides must be short and slow. The way to improve is to make your easy rides easier and your hard rides harder. That way you get both quality rest and quality stress to force your body to improve and give it the time necessary to do so. Too many riders go fairly hard on days that are supposed to be easy. Then they are too tired to go fast on the days set aside for hard training and those days degenerate into only fairly hard ones also. Pretty soon every day is the same and you are plodding towards mediocrity.

So take easy days on Friday and Saturday, before Sunday's race or hard group training ride and after the concentrated work of Tuesday and Thursday. Take another on Monday to be sure you recover from competition. Take it even if you blew the doors off everyone in the race and are so psyched up that you can't wait to train even harder. Patience.

9
Speedwork:
intervals and repeats

Improvement comes when your body
adapts to repeated stress

SPEEDWORK IS the heart and soul of your training, and if you don't do it you won't go as fast as you could. I'm not using the term speedwork in this chapter in quite the same way that road racers do. To them, speedwork involves sharpening their sprint or developing the ability to go 30-35 m.p.h. for fairly short periods of time in order to close a gap. It is developed primarily with all-out training sprints of 100 to 300 meters with enough rest so the heart rate drops to 80 or 90 beats per minute between efforts. Eddie B describes the intensity as "like you are sprinting for the world championship." These lung busters develop flat-out speed over short distances.

While such speed is fine for a time trialist to have, it really isn't necessary. If you have enough left to sprint at the end of a time trial, you have saved too much energy that would have been better used more gradually over the whole race. Sprinting is a spectacular but profligate spendthrift of your body's energy stores because it is a purely anaerobic effort, one that not even the best athlete can keep up for long.

So I'll refer to the kind of speedwork, in a context of time trial training, that raises your steady-state pace a little – perhaps a mile or so per hour – over a month or more of workouts.

Since the aerobic demands of time trialing are similar to those of running, the system advocated by Bill Dellinger, track coach at the University of Oregon, provides a good perceptual framework. Dellinger speaks of "goal pace" and "date pace." Your goal pace is the average speed you want to ride in your best race of the season. For example, if it is now May and your goal is to break the hour in August, your goal pace is 25 m.p.h. Actually it is slightly higher because you have to factor in the effects of the slower start and turnaround on your average speed but we'll discount that relatively minor factor here.

Your date pace, on the other hand, is the speed you can handle for a similar distance right now. So if you did the local 25-mile TT last week in 62:30 your date pace is about 24 m.p.h. Of course you have to take variables like wind and hills on the course into consideration.

Once you know the gap between your current speed and your goal, you can train in a way that accustoms your body to the faster pace. The general rule is that the shorter the training effort, the faster above your goal pace it should be done. For instance, you'd try to do two-mile training time trials slightly above your goal pace – maybe 26 m.p.h. – while in shorter interval workouts you would shoot for perhaps 27 or 28 m.p.h. This accustoms you physically and mentally to greater speeds. If you do all your fast training only at current race pace you won't adapt to greater effort and you'll be unable to produce it in competition.

Remember the training principle of specificity: Your body doesn't like surprises and will only do in a race what you've accustomed it to do in training. Rich Hammen, a former national team member and top racer in the mid '70s, put it succinctly: "It is easier for a fast rider to go slow than for a slow rider to go fast."

So the part of your weekly training that is done at speeds greater than race pace is the part that leads directly to improvement. Everything else is either done to promote endurance (conditioning rides) or is merely filler to keep you loose, stimulate recovery, and burn a few extra calories (easy days).

But don't overdo it. Repeated fast riding is physically tough and can be mentally crushing if you overindulge. Remember that these goal and date pace figures are only guides, as I'll explain in more detail later. What is really important is how you feel, how fast you recover, and whether the workout helps you to improve.

The general rule is to do speedwork a maximum of twice a week and then only for six to eight weeks at a time. Otherwise you'll get stale and stop improving. And remember that a race counts as a speedwork session.

Intensity is important. For instance, it is better to do five or six really demanding intervals in good form once a week than to do three weekly sessions of 10 which, because of exhaustion or lack of concentration, deteriorate to the point that the last several are slow-motion slogs. You won't get better, you'll just get beat – and beaten.

There is no reason to let speedwork get boring or repetitious, because it can take many forms, all useful for a time trialist. In this and the next chapter let's look at how intervals, repeats, training time trials, random jams, group rides, motorpacing, and mass-start racing can help your time trial speed.

Interval training

Interval training is the most precise form of speedwork and many riders feel that it is the most intense and demanding. The theory behind interval training is simple – do a hard effort, rest only long enough to permit partial recovery, and repeat the effort. Scientists say that this increases your body's ability to recover quickly. The value of this training comes during recovery when the body adapts to the demands. The effort phase of the interval is important only in that it sets the stage for the adaptation process to occur during rest.

Coaches who urge you to do intervals don't always come right out and say it, but what you have to recover from if intervals are to be beneficial is plain old exhaustion – time after time. So it is only fair to warn you that intervals make you breathe hard, perspire, and maybe even lose your breakfast. No pain, no gain.

The classic way to do intervals and be sure your recovery period is not too long for maximum benefit is to take your heart rate on the carotid artery just as you do on steady rides. The procedure is to do, for instance, a half-mile jam in a big gear that gets your heart rate up around 180. When your heart rate drops to 120, repeat the half-mile jam. The time required between interval work sessions for your heart rate to drop isn't important although it will decrease as you become fitter and your body adapts to the intervals.

Of course, taking your pulse in this way is a rather cumbersome process. But it doesn't take long to develop a sense of how much time it takes for your heart rate to drop back to the right level. Then it is easier to do your intervals by subjectively monitoring your breathing and your feelings of fatigue.

Electronic heart rate monitors seem to be even less reliable at the

Pacing chart for intervals and repeats											
Speed in mph	20	21	22	23	24	25	26	27	28	29	30
Approx. time/mile in minutes	3:00	2:51	2:44	2:36	2:30	2:24	2:19	2:13	2:08	2:04	2:00

higher heart rates of interval training than they are on steady rides. Still, some cyclists – including LeMond – swear by these devices. They argue that only in this way can they exactly monitor their recovery rates and get the most benefit out of the time spent in intense work.

Another way to do intervals is to specify the time between work efforts, hence the standard interval dose of one minute on, one minute off. Again, you'll have to listen to your body and decide if you need more or less time to get your heart rate down to around 120 b.p.m.

Remember to maintain correct form when you do intervals. Keep a steady, smooth cadence, a good aerodynamic position, and work on your concentration just as in an actual time trial. Don't thrash all over the bike in the final stages of the effort or let your cadence drop below 90. If it does, you are in an excessive gear for the length of the work phase. Don't practice bad habits.

Also stop your interval workout when your time for a given distance deteriorates substantially for two repetitions in a row. Suppose that you planned to do 10 one-mile intervals. You clock 2:16, 2:13, 2:15, and 2:17 for the first through the fourth. Then number 5 is 2:25 and number 6 is 2:31. Stop right there, cool down, and pedal easily home. Once your speed deteriorates, you aren't improving by continuing to force yourself. You are only practicing going slowly.

Some riders arbitrarily determine the number of intervals they plan to do and nothing will stop them from doing them all. While such grim determination is admirable in some circumstances, it is a useless display of grit in training. Better to save both the physical and emotional energy for competition. You'll need it. So be honest with yourself about how you feel because it is a highly individual process. Eddie B warns: "Do what you can handle, do all that you can handle." No more.

One useful interval workout is a decreasing time ladder. For instance, do a 1:30 hard effort so you are anaerobic the last 10 or 15 seconds and can barely keep up your cadence to the end. Then pedal easily until your heart rate drops appropriately, followed by another hard effort. However, shorten the second work phase to 1:20. Repeat, reducing the effort phase 10 seconds each time until it reaches 30 seconds. This compensates for your fatigue and enables you to keep the speed and cadence high.

Repeats

Another way to develop time trial speed is to do repeats. These differ from intervals in that you allow more complete recovery between efforts. They are generally longer too. Keep the pace 2 or 3 miles per hour faster than your current race pace. If you time trial at 24 m.p.h., do these at about 26 m.p.h.

A bicycle computer is useful for these repeats because you know exactly how fast you are going all through the effort. You can do it by figuring total time on a regular stop watch but that way you don't know until the end if the pace was correct. Although bike computers are great on a wind-load simulator, I have several reservations about their use on the road. Aesthetically they clutter up the bike, introducing extra wires and attachments that disrupt its lines. More practically, the monitor can become hypnotic, compelling you to look at it too frequently and take your eyes off the road.

Without a bike computer you can use the time-per-mile chart in this chapter to figure out how fast you are going. Mark the road every half mile on your favorite training route to help you monitor your speed.

Wind or the grade of the road can turn actual road speed into pretty useless information. I often do one-mile repeats on a straight, smooth stretch but can rarely break 2:20 for them. However, like every other road in the valley where I live, this one is slanted uphill especially in the last 200 yards and it goes southwest into the prevailing wind. When I do repeats there I can become pretty discouraged because I can't achieve my goal pace for the workout. Yet I'm working plenty hard just to go 25 m.p.h. in the best conditions. When that Colorado spring wind starts, it is 42x17 all the way.

So the figures flashing on a high tech computer or on your watch need to be interpreted in light of the conditions. Once you have some experience, your own subjective feelings of effort are the best guides to the intensity and value of your workout.

One way to avoid the vagaries of wind and gradient is to find a suitable loop course and use it the same way runners use a track when they do repeat quarter miles. Haserot does workouts at his local airport parking lot at night after the airport is closed, on a ¾-mile loop road. He does one-mile intervals, finding that a half-mile slow recovery in between is about right for him. Before his PR 25-miler of 55:29 he reports that he was doing consistent mile times of around 2:09 for 10 repetitions. This works out to about four seconds per mile faster than his actual race pace, or about one mile per hour faster than he went on his PR ride.

There is another important qualifier on goal and date pace as applied to repeats. Many riders find that even if their date pace for a 10-mile TT is 25 m.p.h., in training they have difficulty exceeding it for shorter repeats. That 25 m.p.h. average that you rode in Saturday's big competition can be impossible to attain the following Tuesday for even one mile at a time despite the added rest. The reason is that the psychological high produced by competition lets you do things you normally couldn't. It is why 100-pound women lift cars off their children or soldiers carry wounded comrades to safety. It is this stimulation of adrenaline that changes "just riding" into a race, with all its potential for allowing you to exceed your normal limits.

So it is important to remember that if you feel like you are going all-out in training you probably are working your body at a rate closer to your maximum than the miles-per-hour figures seem to indicate.

As a more graphic example, consider another sport that relies on precision. When I ran high hurdles, the barriers were 10 yards apart. A hurdler had to be able to take that distance in three strides. I would often find that I had trouble doing so during the week in practice and I began to develop a bad habit of overstriding. It also shook my confidence when I thought about the difficulty I was having. I began to think that the 400-meter event, with its shorter barriers and longer distance between hurdles, was better suited to my stride pattern. Yet I never had any problem getting three balanced, normal-length strides between high hurdles in competition.

Repeated fast riding is physically tough, but that is the part of your weekly training that leads directly to improvement.

It took me awhile to realize that it was the competition-inspired adrenaline that gave me the little extra boost I needed. Once I realized that, I merely moved the hurdles a foot or so closer in practice so I could get the same feel between them that I got in a race while I worked on my form over the hurdle.

In the same way, you may need to reduce your goal and date pace about a mile per hour to take into consideration your lessened emotional readiness in day after day of training conditions.

Wait a minute, you're probably thinking, what good is speedwork if you don't do it all-out? Most riders believe that to get better you have to suffer and to suffer you have to be keyed to a wild-eyed frenzy. Not true. Of course, three or four repeats done half-heartedly won't do you much good. However, it is possible to go hard and work at a high level of physical involvement but stay mentally detached, coolly and objectively analyzing your feelings of fatigue.

Plenty of riders have made the mistake of going out twice a week for two months and throwing heart and soul into their speedwork only to find that they have no psychological fire come race day. It was extinguished in a flood of adrenaline.

Guidelines for speedwork

Longer repeats and intervals are more useful to a time trialist than 30-second bursts. But in general don't make the work phase longer than about one mile. If you do, your speed may drop and the whole purpose is to develop speed and recovery.

Keep your cadence at 90-95 r.p.m. most of the time. This is the generally accepted range for successful time trialing and you should train most of the time at that rate. However, I believe that it helps to increase the cadence to as much as 110 r.p.m. occasionally to give range to your abilities. This carries over directly into competition when there is a strong tailwind or a downhill. It also gives your legs a little variety and this helps you to improve. Many riders know that they get faster if they vary the type of workout. No one does the same interval workout twice a week for eight weeks, but too few riders vary their accustomed pedal cadence.

Choose a gear that will let you pedal the same cadence for the duration of the interval or repeat. If you start at 95 and have bogged down to 80 by the end, the gear is too big or the work phase too long. Besides, struggling at the end only breeds feelings of failure. This is hardly the emotion you want to carry away from your workouts. Train for success.

During the rest period of either intervals or repeats don't stop riding but pedal easily in a lower gear, maintaining a normal cadence. This keeps things moving in your legs and simulates race conditions. It is also easier mentally since there isn't as great a transition from full effort to the lessened effort of the resting phase. To simplify matters, many riders merely shift from the large to the small chainring after each repeat. So if you do the hard work in 53x16 you'd roll around recovering in 42x16.

Although misery loves company, it usually works better to do speedwork by yourself. Time trialing is a solo effort with no one there to push you so it is better to get used to the solitude and the need for self-motivation in training. Also it is hard to find a training partner who is closely matched to you. Even two 59:30 time trialists can differ widely on any given day in their ability to do one-mile repeats. You need to do what you can handle on your hard days, not adjust yourself to someone else's rhythms and emotional state.

If you do speedwork with others, do the efforts side by side. Be sure it is understood that it isn't a race. Each rider should do what he is capable of on that day. Records aren't kept for workouts, only for races.

Choose a suitable stretch of road for your speedwork. For a time trialist a flat or slightly rolling road free of traffic signals is preferable. It should have as few intersections as possible and a wide shoulder to reduce the danger. It should be long enough so you can do several consecutive effort-and-rest combinations going the same direction before you encounter a stop light or dead end.

Finally, do your repeats into the wind as well as with a tailwind. You'll get both in competition and it is best to learn to handle all conditions in training.

10

Speedwork: jams and test TTs

*Spice up your training menu
with these variations*

IN THE LAST chapter I discussed intervals and repeats as a method of gradually raising your steady state pace over weeks and months of training. Another way to increase your speed is to incorporate hard efforts of different lengths over varied terrain into your training ride. These are usually done in a completely unstructured way as the mood hits. Runners call them by the Swedish name "fartlek." To me that sounds like the affliction of a Scandinavian bike racer after a Mexican dinner. So in the interests of better communication, I'll call them random jams. (I know, that sounds like you can't make up your mind what to put on your toast.) But call them whatever name you will, they are the best way to vary your training menu.

I usually warm up for 7-10 miles on the flat, then ride a rolling course. The workout can range from fairly structured to free-form. I often do a predetermined workout, following rules I've made up for myself. They are:

1. Jam hard on every hill.

2. Sprint 100 to 300 meters starting at three or four previously designated mailboxes.

3. Go hard three times, a mile each, on several flat stretches of road.

A less structured workout can still involve rules. For instance:

1. Sprint 100 yards every time you see a bluebird.

2. Try to catch every slow-moving farm vehicle.

3. Jam hard every time you see a patch of glass. (This one can be exhausting in Colorado or any state without a bottle law.)

Like intervals and repeats by the watch, all these rules have their place. But in the best kind of training you just roll along punctuating your steady pace with whatever faster improvisations your mood and the terrain suggest. In rolling country a good rider can sprint up little hills, crank down them to recover, blast out of corners, and sprint against passing traffic. He will be riding with much the same feel for the bumps, gradient and possibilities of the terrain as a downhill skier who works a slope, sometimes doing fast giant slalom turns, sometimes cranking off quick turns in the moguls. On the bike or on skis this is the best kind of training.

The biggest advantage of random jams is that you can do the workouts in a group. Intervals, repeats, and training time trials (which I will discuss next) are best done alone so you can go at your own optimum pace. But in a small, spirited group unstructured speedwork comes naturally. Everyone jams the hills, natural competitiveness surfaces and someone takes a flyer while the rest chase him. The group slows to talk or eat, then there is a little downhill that picks up the speed and several riders will sustain it on the flat with long pulls. And it is a long-standing training tradition to sprint for city limit signs.

Training time trials

As you might expect, training time trials are one of the best methods of getting ready for competition. But there is more to it than just getting out and hammering away once or twice a week.

The first rule is to keep your training time trials short – two miles is ideal – but do several of them. Many riders compete in their local club 10-miler once a week and think that's all the pain they have to endure to make them better. And they will improve – to a point. But a series of short repeated training time trials is a better way.

The first drawback to one all-out weekly training competition is that you only practice the skills of the start, getting up to speed, the turnaround, and the finish once each week. If you do five two-milers, you practice each of those skills five times.

Also, at the shorter distance your speed is higher during each repeat so you accustom yourself to going faster. Yet you build endurance by repeating the process a number of times. As Eddie B observes: "No one needs to train 15 kilometers hard to be able to do 40 hard." This is the same principle as a marathon runner doing repeat miles on the track.

If you do your interval training with another rider, take turns at the front to vary your effort. Or, if one rider is stronger than the other, the slower rider can draft and they can still do the same workouts.

Remember these aren't intervals. You should allow yourself plenty of recovery time between each effort, rolling around in a small gear. Recover so your performance doesn't drop drastically. Try to balance gears, speed, and recovery time so you can do three to five repeats at a similar pace. Don't fall into the trap of doing the first one so hard that you are only going through the motions for the rest. Haserot points out that the "ability to do these workouts with consistent times is a better indication of time trial fitness than actual average times."

As in repeats, try to maintain a pace that is about two miles per hour faster than your current competitive pace over longer distances. Remember that the process of getting started, turning, and re-accelerating will add confounding variables. You may be clocking 25 m.p.h. once you get rolling. In the middle of a longer TT that speed would clock you a 4:48 for two miles. But starting and turning will add quite a few seconds, so judge your speed accordingly.

I often use a practically deserted frontage road next to a four-lane highway to do training time trials. Measure the course accurately with a properly calibrated bike computer or use the highway department's mileage marker stakes. Your start and turnaround should be identified by fairly permanent landmarks – a driveway is better than a shrub or tree.

As in any high-intensity training be sure you are warmed up properly. It is a good idea to go through your regular pre-race warm-up routine, varying it until you find out what works best. I like to do the course once in a lower gear before I actually start timing myself, to complete the warmup process and to check the course for glass, gravel at the turnaround, or potholes that weren't there the last time I rode.

Start from a dead stop just as you would in the real thing. You probably won't be able to talk someone into being a holder but that isn't necessary. Roll slowly up to the line, pause momentarily out of the saddle, then accelerate away just like in a race. If you know how, you can even do a trackstand, balancing on the pedals at the start. These are fun to practice in your living room in the winter when it is too snowy to ride. They may even have some carryover to bike handling skills when you are moving. However, don't waste time practicing them just so you can do one at the start of a training time trial. A momentary pause will do.

Use a digital watch to time yourself. This can be difficult because it's hard to push the button on the watch while you are out of the saddle, poised to uncork a powerful start. Instead, mount the watch on the bars by wrapping a piece of old insole around the bar next to the stem to give it enough thickness to hold the watch. When you start, glance at the time, check it again when you finish, and subtract. It makes these computations easier after the mind-numbing shock of three or four repeats if you plan your start for an even number like 3:20:00.

Prepare the turnaround in advance. You won't have a cone in the middle of the road but a small painted dot will do. To give you advance warning in the absence of other landmarks put three dots 100 yards from the turnaround, two dots at 50 yards, and one dot on the spot. Be sure to check behind and in front for traffic before you hang a 180-degree turn.

Do your training time trials on the appointed day, regardless of weather, so you get used to adverse conditions. If it is windy your times will be slower compared to calm days. But training is the best time to practice making yourself small and slicing through the wind. You will get a good power workout going into the wind and leg-speed development coming back. Don't let rain stop you either. You have to learn how to handle a rain-slickened turnaround.

Have some variety in your program. After several weeks, five repeats of the same course in the same gear can get mentally destructive, especially if you aren't improving much. One way to change the psychological scenery a little is to alternate big and smaller gears. For instance, do the first, third, and fifth time trial in 53x16, the second and fourth in 42x16.

You can also vary the course, finding one with a little roller in the middle to practice your hill techniques. Or do them with another rider of about equal ability, taking turns drafting so that one repeat is hard at the front, the next easier. In fact, if you train with another rider who is slower than you, that rider can draft on you during all your repetitions. You get training time trials, he gets a human motorpace.

Finally, don't force yourself into deep fatigue during these sessions. As in interval training or any race simulations, if you start struggling to maintain your speed over several repeats or if you just don't have it mentally, quit before you dig your hole deeper.

Now what about those local 10-milers I told you to forget? Go ahead and ride them whenever you feel the urge to compete. However, you should view them strictly as competition, not everyday training. Use them as a way to test your race equipment and the results of your shorter, faster training, not as a training device in themselves. "If you are going to make a mistake," cautions Potoff, "have equipment failure, or overextend yourself, it is better to have it happen now than in a really important time trial."

For many racers whose primary interest is fitness and who can't afford the time to travel to distant events, these local time trials are a great way to get good competition frequently. Potoff is a member of a local time trialing club that holds informal time trials almost every other week over varied terrain and distance. Ralph Brandt says, "I ride in a time trial series from April to September that has one 40km competition each month."

11

Speedwork: motorpacing and group riding

The fast pace of these workouts
carries over to solo competition

MOTORPACING is a little-understood training technique that many riders use to prepare for road events, especially time trials. It involves riding behind a vehicle and using its draft so you can maintain higher speeds than you could by yourself.

The classic setup is a small motorcycle with a roller device attached to the rear so the bike rider can get so close that he occasionally touches his front wheel to the roller. It would be a disaster if the bike's front wheel touched the rear wheel of the motorcycle or some stationary part of it, but with a roller nothing happens.

It is also possible to motorpace behind larger motorcycles, a car, or a van. Motorcycles over about 250cc don't run smoothly at the 25-35 m.p.h. that is right for most motorpacing. They tend to leave you on little hills and it is hard for the driver to keep a steady pace on the flat. Cars and vans compound the problem but they provide more draft so you can stay back further than you can behind a motorcycle for added safety.

Why does motorpacing help you time trial? Can't you just ride hard, fighting the wind, and get the same benefit? Some riders believe so. They don't motorpace because they want to duplicate the demands of the race in training. Brandt speaks for this view when he says, "I don't motorpace much since that is not how you race." It is certainly possible to be a fine time trialer, as Brandt is (a sub-55-minute PR), without motorpacing.

Advocates of motorpacing cite several advantages. First, they maintain, it increases your speed because you'll go faster behind the motor and that speed will carry over to unpaced competition. For this reason, national team riders use motorpacing frequently in their training for road events. Eddie B recommends strongly that many of the interval and repeat workouts for individual and team time trialists be motorpaced.

Twigg has benefitted from this program and says, "We do quite a bit of motorpacing during the season. It gets you used to going fast. [Then] when you are by yourself you feel like you should be going faster." Susan Ehlers agrees. "I think motorpacing is very effective for time trial training. It allows you to ride a big gear for a longer time than you normally would"

Olavarri says her preparation for time trials generally consists of motorpacing and steady, flat riding. "I'll do three or four days a week of training behind a motorcycle at 25-30 m.p.h. for two to three weeks prior to the event."

Another reason to motorpace is that it is possible to control the speed, and hence your effort, very tightly with the motor acting as a pacer. On a flat road the driver can increase speed one mile per hour every 10 minutes or so. This enables you to remain at your anaerobic threshold for long periods of time because the effort is steady. The motor also is a psychological advantage because it acts like a rabbit. You don't have to think about anything except following that vehicle. That means more of your energies can go into the physical part of training. If you have a coach, he can drive the motorcycle or car and keep close watch and even control your progress.

Because it increases speed, motorpacing is the ideal final preparation a week or so before a time trial. Casebeer says, "It will help polish. It makes you go a little faster." An experienced time trialist like Hammer advises: "The week before, motorpace two or three times – a one-hour workout after a one- or two-hour warmup ride."

The best motorpacing terrain is relatively flat on lightly traveled roads with few intersections. Try to choose a smooth road, because it is hard to see oncoming potholes until they are right under your front wheel. On wide roads a motorcycle and following cyclist can get over on the shoulder out of the way of passing cars. If you ride behind a car on narrow country roads it should have an emergency flasher going to warn overtaking traffic.

That brings up two things about motorpacing that may cause you to reject it: It is dangerous and, in some states, it may be illegal.

The danger is obvious. Speeds are higher, so any crash is going

Riding in the draft of a motorcycle gets you used to going faster, longer, in a bigger gear.

to be more dangerous for that fact alone. Also you have a metal vehicle right in front of your nose. If it stops abruptly or swerves, it's
a much more painful object to hit than another rider on a bike. A
motorpacing vehicle also goes slower than other road users, so some
disruption of traffic flow with its attendant dangers is inevitable.

I checked with the local office of the Colorado State Highway Patrol on two occasions and it was the opinion of both officers I talked
to that motorpacing was illegal. The charge would be "following too
closely" or drafting, the same violation as a car drafting on a semi.
I don't know how the law reads in your state or whether the local
authorities would choose to enforce it. At the Olympic Training
Camp in Colorado Springs coaches have told me that sometimes
they are ticketed while on other days officers cruise by uncon-
cerned.

Given the muddy legal situation, I've felt in the past that motorpacing wasn't an unethical action because you would be jeopardiz-
ing only yourself, not other road users. However, the disruption of
traffic flow is a consideration and the danger is certainly a major
factor, legalities aside.

If your goal is fitness and you don't want a serious injury that
would temporarily or permanently keep you from cycling, motorpacing may be an unjustifiable risk. Like other safety issues in cycling
or any other sport it is a personal decision that only you can make
in light of your own priorities.

Because it's like a fast pace line with short hard pulls, team time trialing is ideal speed-work for the individual time trial. Aerodynamically equipped right down to the water bottles and cages, this Soviet team set a world record of 53.7 k.p.h. in the 1985 world championships.

Alternatives to motorpacing

You can get the same benefit of motorpaced workouts in legal and safer ways than by following a motor. Quite a few national-class riders have been using many of these techniques the last several years and find that they work well.

One method is to use a strong tailwind. When those spring winds I mentioned blow at 20-40 m.p.h. I'll ride with them, spinning a 53x13 on the flat. The speed, effort, and proximity to my anaerobic threshold are all nearly equivalent to a motorpaced ride. The drawback is that you'll need someone to pick you up at the end of the downwind tack. You don't want a leg-deadening grind home if the purpose of the workout is speed development.

This disadvantage can be overcome by incorporating the ride into some other aspect of your life. I often ride those southwest spring breezes 40 or 50 miles northeast, meet my wife and son, and we hike or crosscountry ski for the afternoon. Or a group of four or five fast riders could trade off every 10 miles or so to drive a car out for the return trip.

If you live in hilly or mountainous country, long gradual downhills work just as well. I am fortunate to be surrounded by varied terrain so that a wind-assisted ride to the northeast is basically flat while to the east there is a 14-mile uphill. I often ride up there, working on power on the climb, and then fly back in big gears for speed. True, the climb constitutes some slow miles but it comes first in the ride so the leg speed I get on the return trip seems to be what stays with me.

Group rides, whether in training or in mass-start racing, may be the best motorpace substitute as well as an excellent developer of leg speed in their own right. Even if you are a solitary trainer and a time trial specialist it is worth your while to arrange your schedule so you can ride with a fast group regularly. Potoff lives in Tucson, a center of cycling activity, and reports that he has a few friends "who are capable of riding so fast that you actually simulate both motorpacing and intervals."

Hammer says he gets ready for time trials by developing "road fitness acquired by frequent and long road races." Many leading women racers compete in men's events because the effect of riding in a pack of faster riders is like motorpacing.

You don't need a big group, either. Two to four are plenty. In fact, a small group can get more intense work by doing team time trials. Besides being an event in itself, team time trials are ideal speedwork for individual time trial events.

Basically team time trialing is like a fast pace line with riders taking short but very hard pulls at the front. With two riders, limit pulls to about 25 seconds but go hard. You'll get very little rest that way and plenty of interval-like efforts at the front. Two strong, competitive people can ride themselves into the ground in 10 miles doing this and it is ideal preparation about a week before the event.

And remember that the best time trialists are, almost without exception, strong all-round riders. They compete in road races, criteriums, stage races, and possibly on the track. They have general racing fitness and, with specific time trial sharpening, they have an advantage over the time trial specialist.

12
Overtraining

Learn to recognize the symptoms
and know how to prevent them

I AM DEVOTING a whole chapter to the subject of overtraining because it has destroyed plenty of careers. Too little training means that you'll never reach your potential but you will always enjoy the sport and come back for more. Overtraining, on the other hand, ruins your enthusiasm for the bike. Too much training and you'll hate the thought of a workout and dread the prospect of a race. It will poison your delight.

You probably wouldn't be doing such an individual, strenuous, and relatively unknown sport as bike racing if you weren't strongly self-motivated to succeed. The type of personality which believes, consciously or not, in the Protestant work ethic — the harder you work, the better you get — is in danger of overtraining. The Puritans would have been turkeys on the bike. If you are a workaholic on the job, there is no reason to believe that you'll approach time trialing any differently.

In order to understand overtraining you need to understand the general adaptation syndrome (GAS), named by pioneering stress researcher Hans Selye. Some stress can be positive, like training. In its presence your body adjusts to increasing demands and becomes stronger. You gradually become able to handle larger and larger stress loads if you allow enough time between stresses so you recover. This is what happens when you add intervals gradually to your training program or ride 10% more each week until you are able to do twice the mileage you previously thought possible. On the other hand, if the stress load is too large or if stresses come too frequently, the body can't adapt and exhaustion follows. A paradox: More training will make you slower.

In addition, stress is cumulative. What you do in training is only part of the equation. You have to consider all the stress you are subjected to daily from your job, family, studies, and physical surroundings when you analyze the effect of a workout on your recovery. This is one reason that world-class athletes are so good. They do little but train, thus reducing other stresses that might detract from the adaptive process.

Also, adaptation is specific. Your adaptive energy is limited. Applying a particular stress like training strengthens you in relation to that stress but weakens you in relation to all others. That is why it's difficult to gain endurance at the same time you gain speed or why, just when you start improving on the bike, you come down with a cold. The general adaptation syndrome is a finite, limiting mechanism.

Recognize the symptoms

The first step in avoiding overtraining is to keep a training diary. A diary is absolutely essential to help you spot patterns in the varied overtraining symptoms you may experience. You can use a diary published especially for cycling or sports, or you can just use a notebook. What is important is that year after year you keep a consistent record of your training, your objective physical parameters like body weight, and your subjective feelings of fatigue or vigor. My diary dates back to March 1975 without a break and is invaluable in helping me decide what works and what doesn't.

Next, learn to recognize overtraining by being alert for a number of symptoms, mild and unimportant separately, that mean trouble when three or four appear at once.

1. A dangerous symptom is *persistent fatigue,* especially throbbing legs that keep you awake or ache when you do mild exercise like climbing stairs. A tired, washed-out feeling that continues from day to day is not as obvious but equally important. If you are too tired to mow the lawn, you shouldn't be training.

2. *Delayed-action fatigue.* If you ride hard on Sunday and come home hyper – unable to fall asleep that night because you are too wired up – but feel drowsy and lethargic on Monday and nearly catatonic on Tuesday, watch out. Abnormally slow recovery or fatigue that deepens in spite of rest means that you are no longer adapting to your total stress.

3. *Rapid weight loss.* Once you have good aerobic fitness and your weight has stabilized, sudden drops mean either that you haven't rehydrated from a hot ride or that your reserves are so low that

your body is feeding on itself, using muscular tissue for energy. Both are signs to back off. Quite a few muscular, stocky riders with low body fat percentages want to be thinner so they restrict their caloric intake. They are pleased when their weight drops but they don't realize that what they have lost isn't fat but rather the muscle that propels them down the road.

Eddie B was once asked at a clinic what he thought about fasting. "Not eat?" he said incredulously. "Bike racing is hard work!" So eat a balanced diet with plenty of carbohydrates and your muscles will have fuel to burn. Even if your weight loss is merely fluid because of a hot ride, you need to take it easy in training until you rehydrate. You won't go any faster on an empty radiator than you will on an empty fuel tank. Riding on empty is a major stress that your body doesn't need.

4. *Disrupted sleep patterns.* It is called depression insomnia. You are exhausted in the evening, fall asleep easily, but wake at 4 or 5 a.m. and stare at the ceiling. By 10 a.m. you are ready for a nap. Any disruption of your normal sleep rhythm means that your body is trying to tell you something. Listen.

5. *A breakdown of your body's ability to fight disease.* If you get one cold after another, too much of your energy has been used in training with little left over to ward off infection. Persistent saddle sores, chronic cold sores, road rash that doesn't heal even if it has been properly treated, all are signs that your body's defense mechanisms have been overloaded.

6. *Abnormal lack of enthusiasm for training and racing.* Perhaps you have noticed a feeling of depression, mild to fairly severe, after extended hard racing or a difficult period of training. This is depression in the literal sense – not just a pervasive sense of melancholy but also a general slowing down of your functions. You may be slower when you walk, clumsy at small tasks, not as quick to see connections, jokes, or nuances of meaning in the remarks of others. You'll probably be grouchy, irritable, and hard to be around.

You are also likely to be uninterested in training and dread the thought of a race. You may become fearful about potential crashes in group rides or road races, dwelling obsessively on the dangers and visualizing gory crashes in your mind, with yourself as the victim. Overtraining can create a depression that literally changes your personality, making you more fearful and less in synchronization with the world you inhabit.

If your performance is getting worse instead of better you may be training too hard.

7. The most telling signal of all: *deteriorating performances in training and racing.* If you are getting worse instead of better despite hard training, you are almost certainly getting worse because of that hard training. Check your times in competition as well as in training time trials and repeats. Note them in your diary and watch for steady declines or precipitous plunges.

West of my town there is a rolling three-mile course where I have timed myself over the years as a way of gauging my progress. On July 25, 1982, I rode my best time ever there and four days later I knocked off another four seconds. The Mount Evans Hillclimb was coming up so I continued to do hard riding. Soon I was cooked but wouldn't admit it. A week before Mount Evans I timed myself on the same course again. It was incredibly painful, far more so than on the previous record rides. As I crossed the three-mile mark and punched the watch I was sure that if I had hurt that much, I must have blown my record away. Then I looked at the time – 27 seconds slower. Overtraining had blown me away. Needless to say, on Mount Evans, the mountain won.

8. But where, you may ask, is *elevated resting heart rate* in this hierarchy of symptoms, since it is the one usually thought to be the most important indicator of all? Many coaches suggest that you take your heart rate every morning under similar conditions – lying in bed immediately after you wake is the usual recommendation. Then you are supposed to record the figure in your training diary and look for patterns.

According to many authorities, a reading of 10% higher than normal means that you haven't recovered from yesterday's ride and you should ease off or cancel your training that day. In fact, resting heart rate has been elevated to the status of oracle and some riders not only reduce their workout load at the tiniest fluctuation, they brush their teeth less vigorously too.

I wish it were that easy to spot overtraining. It is tempting to make a fetish out of morning heart rate, with its promise of mathematical precision. But the sad truth for a substantial percent of riders is that sudden increases alone just aren't reliable symptoms of overstress and slowed recovery. Nor are low readings necessarily evidence of good form. Top riders at equal stages of fitness have heart rates that vary from the 30s to the 70s. To add to the confusion, severe chronic fatigue sometimes causes resting heart rate to drop, the opposite of what you would expect.

So, although for some riders this reading has predictive value, the morning ritual of the laying on of hands to wrist often has little practical significance. Try it for six weeks or so to discover if it works for you in combination with the other signs I mentioned earlier. But, generally speaking, there is no magic in resting heart rate fluctuations.

Preventive measures

Knowing all these symptoms of overtraining is helpful only in retrospect however. Once you have spotted them, it is too late. The bear has you. You have to back way off, preferably beginning with several days to a week of complete rest depending on the severity and depth of your fatigue. Then you'll have to start all over again from a lower state of fitness. Learning by experience isn't much fun and exacts a heavy penalty. It is what the poet Byron called "a kind of income tax laid on by fate."

So it is important to avoid similar disasters by understanding how to do enough training to adapt and improve without overstressing the general adaptation mechanism. Here are some guiding principles to keep you in the saddle and on the way to your goals:

1. *Moderation.* The 1975 national time trial champion and a dominant figure in road racing in the late 1970s, Wayne Stetina says it best: "It is better to be undertrained than overtrained." When you are rested there is always the possibility of having a great day when it all comes together. These peaks are the result of moderate, regular training and the emotional energy that comes from denying yourself hard training occasionally so you are eager to compete.

Conversely, when you are overtrained, these great performances are rare because most of your emotional energy goes into training to exhaustion and then dragging yourself around through the demands of the rest of the day. What you get is the frequent dismal performance instead of an occasional great one. The progression is inexorably downward.

If you feel a little tired and are in doubt about the kind of training you should do on a certain day, err on the side of prudence. You don't have to invest all your energy into training. If you have some energy capital left for everyday activities off the bike, that's great. Don't train so hard that you bankrupt the rest of your life. In *The Serious Runner's Handbook*, Tom Osler says something that should be inscribed in red capital letters on a poster next to your bike: "When we feel good, look good, and are alert and productive, our bodies are adapting to the stresses (like cycling) which we place upon them. If we feel tired . . . and washed out, we need rest not stress."

2. *Patience.* Progress in training is cyclical and periodic. You'll have ups and downs in performance that don't seem to be related to the training you have been doing. It takes time for the body to adapt to training stresses and your body can't be rushed. It will take its own sweet time and if you push it it will bite back hard.

Because patience is a virtue that no one has ever accused me of having, I've read extensively about Eastern religion and ways of seeing. I wanted to discover if I could find the roots of the patience and acceptance of the way things are that characterize many of these belief systems. In Fritjof Capra's *The Tao of Physics* I found this: "The Chinese believe that whenever a situation develops to its extreme, it is bound to turn around and become its opposite. This basic belief has given them courage and perseverance in times of distress and has made them modest and cautious in times of success. . . . Each time the two forces (which the Chinese call yin and yang) reaches its extreme, it contains within itself the seeds of the opposite. . . . In the Chinese view it is better to have done too little than too much."

In training this means that when you are working your way back to fitness after a restful (or slothful) winter or a forced layoff due to injury you carry the potential for great achievement. You are rested and your emotional energy is at a high level. But when you feel snappy on every ride, when you jam all the hills out of sheer joy, when you want to do intervals four times a week, when you just set a PR, you are only a few pedal strokes away from exhaustion, loss of enthusiasm, and a long layoff.

The best place to be is on the upward swing – moving in the right direction – but never doing so much that you exhaust yourself and tip the cycle in the other direction. According to Capra, the Chinese say that when you are patient and cautious you "won't get very far but you'll be headed in the right direction." In time trialing you may get very far indeed but it will be a slower, progressive movement with long sloping peaks, not low sharp peaks and deep, deep valleys.

3. *Recognize your limitations.* Everyone has upper limits to how fast he can ride. We are limited by our genetic potential, trapped in the cage of our own bodies. We differ from world champions in this respect only in the height of those limits. But, regardless of your talent, the closer you come to your potential, the harder it is to improve. Faster times come in smaller and smaller increments for a given volume of work. Yet you are so near your goal that you try even harder with more racing, more intervals, more emotional energy poured into the sport. At this point you are likely to get worse instead of better as your body is overwhelmed by the stress. Balladeer Paul Simon understands the paradox inherent in training: "The nearer your destination, the more you're slip-slidin' away."

4. *Learn to accept the limits of your total stress load.* If you have a job, schooling, or a family all making demands on your time and energy you have to be very careful of increasing your training load. You have heard all the training formulas: The East German riders do 15,000 miles a year, last year's U.S. national champion motorpaced four times the week before his victory, the rider who lives down the street does 300 miles a week rain or shine. But every one

of those riders has a unique set of personal circumstances and a highly individual ability to adapt. The simplistic idea that you could be so much better if only you could ride more and faster miles is hopelessly naive in light of the complex balancing act between priorities and time that most riders have to do.

True confession time. In 1982 I was going well in the early season. Flushed with success I drove the 500-mile round trip from my home to road and stage races near Denver several weekends in a row. During the week I continued to train hard hoping to peak for the district time trial. But the effort of hard racing and training coupled with the stress of job, family, and travel led me into a bad case of overtraining.

Two weeks before the TT rolled around I lacked snap on the bike and had to force myself to train. I felt tired all the time and was an irritable grouch at home. I refused to acknowledge it even to myself although all the danger signs were flashing like neon before my eyes. My wife took to telling me, gently, that I was about as much fun to be around as a bear with colic.

As so often happens in chronic fatigue of this sort, I not only lost my physical edge on the bike but found that my central nervous system functions were dulled too. I stumbled around in a kind of doddering haze. At home I would get up to do an errand in the next room, only to forget the chore by the time I arrived. I became clumsy, dropping my toothbrush in the toilet bowl and fumbling with buttons. Small everyday objects developed a mind and will of their own. I became slightly paranoid as inanimate objects like footstools and my son's toys, that I had gotten along with beautifully for years, suddenly became the enemy lurking on the floor or stairs waiting to trip me up.

When I showered after a ride, my sweat smelled like an ammonia factory. Our shower has a seat. This was a good thing because I was too exhausted to stand. In the evening I plopped amoeba-like into a reclining chair and sprawled there in a torpor as my metabolism shut down to conserve what little energy I had left. Now I know what a hibernating woodchuck feels like.

I should have known that what I needed was a long rest off the bike. What I did was more intervals on Thursday, another six-hour stint in the car on Saturday, and an all-out effort in the TT on Sunday in the hope (a vain one, as it turned out) of setting a new PR.

So moderation in training coupled with self-knowledge are the real keys to success in time trialing, not day after day of flagellating yourself on the bike into a state of incompetence. Contrary to popular belief, it is precariously easy to train hard. Just go out each day, hunker down on a big gear, and crank till you croak. Then do it again. Nothing could be simpler. It doesn't take genius to train this way, only commitment.

Unfortunately, success doesn't come that easily. Sure, you have to put in the physical work. But planning the workouts and monitoring your body are even more important. Only you can be responsible for the harmony among your training components, cleverly playing long rides against shorter ones, hard intervals in counterpoint with easy rides, flat-out competitive efforts *fortissimo*, rest days *sotto voce*. In this way the crafty rider fine tunes his training volume and intensity: not too little, never too much.

13
Peaking and tapering

The balance between rest and work
is crucial before important events

YOUR TRAINING is complete. You've put in your time day after day in all kinds of weather, going hard when you had to and critically monitoring your body at every step of the way. Competition is your reward: a time to test yourself and your training program both against the clock and against other riders.

How often should you compete? European professionals may race 150 times a season. During stage races like the Tour de France they ride up to 170 miles a day for weeks on end, over difficult terrain in all weather. Top pros can adapt to the demands of daily hard effort, often at the limits of human performance. Their recuperative powers are amazing and are in part due to training, in part to a genetic selection process. Amateur racers who don't have the innate ability necessary for fast recovery don't become pros. Or they don't stay in the cash ranks long.

But time trialing is different from mass-start road racing. It is foolish to claim that any one discipline in bike racing is harder than another – top riders go all out regardless of the event. But even for seasoned road racers time trials are extremely difficult to ride and recover from for a number of reasons. For one thing they are hard all the way with no letup. A 25-mile TT means 25 miles of effort close to your maximum. There is no drafting, no soft-pedaling on the flats, no coasting down hills. The rhythm of a road race is periodic: fast, then a little slower.

When the crunch comes in a road race you'll have to go much faster than you'll go in an individual time trial. But there are periods of relative relaxation punctuating these high-speed jams. So a crafty rider in a mostly flat 100-mile road race might go really hard only for five or 10 miles during the race.

Time trialing is done in a big gear and at a fairly low cadence compared to road racing. This combination tends to deaden your legs and they will recover more slowly than from higher-cadence spinning in a pack. As Hammer says, "Time trials, because of the high gears used, can quickly drain even very fit riders."

Good road and criterium racers know the trick of spinning a moderate gear in the shelter of the pack to save their legs. Your breathing may sound like a water buffalo doing wind sprints when you are spinning that 53x17 at 110-120 r.p.m. but it doesn't affect your legs like muscling a 53x13 at 90 or 95 on your own in a time trial.

Finally, time trials are mentally demanding. Eddie B cautions, "Too many time trials can hurt your psychology. This is a very tough event." You have no pack to ride in, no one's wheel right in front of you to hang on to when the action heats up, no race tactics to consider, no dangermen from other teams to mark. If you are going to go fast it will be because you mentally discipline yourself to do so, not because someone is away on a break and you are hammering in the chase group, your pain forgotten in the excitement of the chase. "I find that a full-effort longer time trial is extremely taxing," maintains Hammer. "More so than long road races or even stage races."

For all these reasons, be extremely careful of competing too often in time trials. Many riders have tried to ride a competitive local club event on Thursday evening, do training time trials alone on Tuesday, and race on the weekend too. In most cases their desire to compete dies a slow and agonizing death over three or four weeks until they are just going through the motions. If you race all the time, you will never be able to really peak for one or two great efforts each season.

This sort of prudence isn't an indication of weakness. Even a star like Twigg says, " I think it is best not to ride so many time trials because they hurt so much." And Olavarri adds, "I really don't like to ride time trials because they are so painful. But I would ride more if they were emphasized more because I seem to do well at them."

Ration your racing so that you are eager to compete, keyed up at the thought of going hard, enthused about putting forth the kind of effort needed to break your PR. If you've raced so much that you find yourself saying "I'll just ride this one for training" then you shouldn't be racing. Why do it if you aren't ready to go all out?

To be ready for your best effort on race day, carefully balance rest and work in the two weeks before.

First, exhaust yourself

Your training in the two weeks before an important event is critical. It involves an even more precise balance between rest and work than is the case in normal training. It is too late to improve, so work that is too intense will leave you tired and without snap on the big day. Do too little all week and you can lose your emotional intensity and your physical edge.

Eddie B is vastly experienced in the fine art of bringing riders to their peaks for races. He recommends initiating the tapering procedure with several days of intense work about a week to 10 days before the time trial. This hard work can be intervals, stage races, or long rides. The purpose of doing two or even three successive days of high-intensity work about a week and a half before your big event is to get your body more tired than normal. Then, if you have timed it right, it will supercompensate by recovering to a higher level of readiness and fitness.

For most riders, Eddie suggests two or three consecutive days of one- to two-mile intervals in a big gear at your normal competitive cadence. Do as many as you can, stopping only when your performance drops significantly for two efforts in a row.

Concentrate on your aerodynamic riding position. Be smooth and steady. These hard interval days are designed to simulate the actual competitive situation and you want to practice what you'll do in the race. Eddie recommends that your coach or another rider watch you during these intervals to be sure that your form stays perfect.

Top European and American road racers use a variation on this technique to get ready for one-day events. The preferred method is to substitute for the intervals a hard stage race of about five days duration that ends about 10 days before the event. Fairly flat races are preferred because the rider's leg speed will be greater. Too much climbing and they get what Eddie calls "slow miles" that may take some snap out of their legs and be a handicap in road races.

Again, the timing of the stage race and the intensity of the stages are both crucial. Before the 1984 Olympics, Eddie and the rest of the national coaching staff agonized over whether to send the Olympic team to the Coors Classic with its 11 stages and substantial climbing or to opt for a shorter, flatter, easier race. (They entered, but some dropped out before the finish.) These decisions are never easy and you don't know if you were right until it is too late to change the results.

Another way to force your body to deplete and then compensate is to take several long hard rides instead of the intervals. If you have been doing speedwork regularly, a 100-miler may be a difficult shock to your system and will take more out of you than faster repeats or intervals. Brandt posted a 54:26, breaking his PR by several minutes, after just such a routine.

Some riders use other high-stress workouts instead of intervals to kick off their taper. Phinney, whose frequent fast criterium racing gives him plenty of speed, says, "I look at time trialing as being like climbing. The stronger the better. I like to take mountain rides to develop strength." Other riders swear by long, fast motorpaced rides. Eddie B says that the intervals he recommends can be done behind a motor if they are lengthened from one or two miles to three or four.

Training time trials are good, but remember that a series of shorter ones will be faster and more beneficial than one 10-miler each day. They will be easier on your head too, and you'll be less likely to leave your desire to go hard out on the road where you train.

Now take it easy

Regardless of your preferred method the whole point is to exhaust yourself about 10 days before the race, then recover with active rest. After the back-to-back hard training, you'll be tired. Roll around easily for a couple of days so you recover.

The week before D-day, Eddie suggests that you follow your normal training routine but cut both mileage and effort by 30%. If you normally do 30 miles and five or six hard repeats on Tuesday, cut to about 20 miles, reduce hard efforts to only three or four, and reduce their distance proportionally. On Friday spin out an easy 15 miles using your race wheels, clothing, and equipment. Saturday do the same but include one or two fairly short race-pace efforts – half a mile at the most. Follow this program, Eddie says, and you will be ready for your best effort on race day.

Of course every rider will react in a different way to any standard tapering plan. Eddie's is a useful guideline but here, as in all aspects of racing, you have to determine what works best for you. If you have been racing frequently and you are tired, that intense series of back-to-back interval days may put you so deeply in the hole that you won't recover by race day. Or maybe the emotional drain of successive hard days will leave you mentally flat and unprepared to accept the level of suffering it will take to ride well. Know yourself.

One problem with intervals is that they can be addictive. One hard day leads to another and pretty soon you're cooked and the race is two days away. Some riders just can't seem to go easy even on scheduled easy days. They start out in 42x19 and soon they are pounding away in the big ring driven by the seductive thrill of speed or by guilt at not putting out 100% all the time. Sometimes only a change of scene will help. Potoff says, " I force myself not to go out on Saturday [before a race] but ride rollers instead so I can stay loose."

As the race nears, it is good to think about it, mentally going through all the time trial techniques from start to finish. Visualize in a positive way the performance you hope to pull off. This is a good time to use the relaxation and positive imagery techniques that sports psychologists recommend and which I'll describe in a later chapter.

Be sure that your pre-race anticipation is positive. Some riders dwell on the pain of the event instead of on techniques or on success. Dreading the pain before a race wastes energy, because a full-blown case of dread is hard work. It also instills all sorts of negative thoughts in your mind that will make you less able to deal with the pain when it does appear.

If you are anticipating the race and you visualize impending pain positively — as effort, as proof that you are going fast, as a challenge to be overcome — then you are mentally ready for an outstanding effort. But if all you see in your mind's eye when you visualize your next competition is lung-burning agony then either you are too overtrained to ride well or for some personal reason you really don't want to do what has to be done to do well.

So there is no reason to suffer the slings and arrows of the anaerobic threshold half a dozen times in your imagination before the event. Once, in the actual race, is plenty. Shakespeare said it: "A coward dies a thousand times before his death, the valiant only taste of death but once."

The stage race TT

A time trial that requires special preparation is the one that happens during a stage race. These time trials can have a big effect on general classification because of the possibility of large time differentials. The strong rider who can't get away from a whole pack of wheelsuckers or who has a weak team so he has to do inordinate amounts of work just to control breaks, can get precious seconds in a time trial because it is every rider for himself.

Because time trial stages are so important, smart riders prepare for them by conserving energy in the events on the day or two before. You'll have to go with threatening breaks but don't initiate them and don't work hard in one. Use lower gears and spin in the pack. Try to ride the hills steadily, get through corners with the leaders so you won't have to sprint to catch up, don't let gaps open that you'll have to work hard to close. Of course, these stages will still be plenty tough. But the idea is to conserve as much energy as possible, then do the time trial all-out.

Remember that five-time Tour de France winner Anquetil won primarily on his ability against the clock. More recent dominant stage racers like Merckx and Hinault have been top time trialers too.

14
Warming up
*Riders differ on how much to do
but all agree it's essential*

"THE WARMUP is the most important factor in being able to turn a good time trial." Potoff says it and it is advice worth listening to because he has some pretty imposing time trial credentials. His assessment of the importance of the warmup comes from years of experience, experimentation, and the knowledge that a time trial is a race that goes hard from the start. You have to be ready for maximum effort as soon as the holder lets go. If you plan to warm up by gradually increasing the pace in the first quarter of the race, you'll never make up the lost time.

Many road riders have trouble making this transition. Twigg explains, "In a time trial you don't have the time like in a road race where the whole pack spins for a few miles." Kiefel adds, "Whatever you do, you have to be completely warmed up before you start — sweating like a pig." So heed the advice of these fast riders. What you do in the hour before the race is at least as important as anything you do during it.

Wear long tights during the warmup. If you're in a skinsuit, roll the top down around your waist, and wear a wool jersey or warmup top. That way when you are ready to race, the top of your skinsuit will be dry instead of soaked with perspiration.

How long to warm up
The length of the warmup depends on your individual preferences, training, and abilities. You need to be loose and ready to go at maximum output but you don't want to be tired. Nor do you want to feel great at the start but fade in the last five miles because of the length or intensity of your pre-race activities.

Generally the more miles you ride in training, the longer your warmup can be. The 7-Eleven team races 60-mile criteriums, 100-mile road races, and members put in 300-400 weekly training miles.

Phinney says that "long fast warmups seem to work very well for
me. At the 1983 Pan Am trials the 7-Eleven team always rode 30
miles to the course."

Potoff is another advocate of riding to the event and says that it
usually takes him 25-30 miles just to get loosened up. Although
Potoff competes in the 35- to 39-year-old age bracket he does nearly
as many miles as younger national-class riders. It isn't unusual for
him to put in 350 miles the week of a time trial.

If you ride shorter training miles, cut down the length of your
warmup. Twigg says her whole warmup takes about half an hour.
This reflects her training pattern, dictated by the shorter distances
of women's racing in general.

Although riding to the race is a good way to warm up, it has its
drawbacks. You don't want to ride your lightweight race tires and
wheels through potholes and glass-strewn streets. So you'll need a
support vehicle tagging along to carry your race wheels and personal belongings and to help out if you have a flat or mechanical
trouble. That is fine if you have a team van but most riders are less
well supported.

If you have driven 200 miles to the race by yourself, don't ride 30
miles from your motel room to the start. If you have a couple of flats
or your derailleur jams you could be sitting by the side of the road
when your start is called. Instead, drive to the course and warm up
back and forth on a two-mile stretch of road near your car. Then if
you have a problem, you'll be closer to help.

I know one local rider, a newcomer to Denver at the time, who
rode to our Colorado district TT course that was about 30 miles from
his home. He took a wrong turn, got lost, and missed the race completely. His 30-mile warmup turned into a 100-mile odyssey in
search of familiar landmarks.

Timing is crucial. If you ride to the race and arrive too early you
have lost the benefits of the warmup and will have to start all over.
Potoff has another method besides riding to the race that he uses
to eliminate the problem. "I arrive by car at a race site at least an
hour ahead of time. I register and find my start time. Then I take
a watch with me and head out to warm up about 35-40 minutes.
When I return I hop on a set of rollers for about 12 minutes. If everything is going according to schedule I get off the rollers with only
two or three minutes to spare." The big advantage of rollers is that
you are warming up but not going anywhere. So it is easy to time
the warmup to the minute.

There are other advantages to warming up on rollers. You won't puncture your lightweight time trial tires or knock a wheel out of true on a pothole. You won't pick up bits of glass to cause a flat five miles into the race. There won't be any traffic to contend with. If it is raining, suspend a tarp between a couple of cars and stay dry until the start. If it is cold, you won't have the cooling effect of moving air so you'll warm up faster. Remember how you sweat on your wind-load simulator in the winter?

Regardless of the length of your warmup or whether you do it all on the road or finish on rollers, the actual procedure is pretty much standard. Twigg sums it up: "I ride easy and then just do some jams – past the point where it starts to hurt but not 100% – for 30 seconds or so, a couple of times. Then a few jumps just to get moving."

Kiefel says, "If it is a [short] time trial I do 10-12 short jumps. If it is a longer TT, I motorpace for 10 miles and do a couple hard pulls to set my tempo and speed for the day." Olavarri adds, "I need a very strong warmup always. I take 45 minutes just riding easy and gradually harder until, 20 minutes before my start, I do three or four short intervals, 400-600 yards, in race gear. I also practice two starts from a slow roll in the gear I plan to start in."

What gears for your warmup? Most riders start out spinning in the small ring and gradually increase gears and speed. Be sure that you spend a fairly substantial portion of your warmup in larger gears though, because that's what you'll be using in the race.

Sipay, commenting on time trialists he observed on a U.S. national team trip to Europe, says that "the pros we saw warming up for time trials in the Tour de l'Avenir never used a little gear. Oh, they might ride the first couple of miles in one but then they'd be rolling around in the big ring at 70 r.p.m. getting the legs accustomed to it."

Some variations

There are additions to the standard warmup that some riders find useful. One is stretching. Shumway says, "I stretch my leg muscles, neck and back." Resh does some stretching for about five minutes, he says, "mainly for the hamstrings." They aren't in a majority, however. Twigg confesses that "stretching probably isn't a bad idea but I don't do it."

If you use stretching movements as part of your normal training, continue them before and after a time trial. If you don't, right before competition is a poor time to begin. I find that a series of stretches for my lower back feels good and keeps me from getting as sore and tight in that area during a race. It is not readily apparent but the powerful muscles of the lower back get heavy use in big-gear pushing whether in flat time trials or climbing. A little stretching before the event seems to delay the feeling that some sadistic soul is at work back there with a blunt instrument.

Another useful variation to your warmup procedure is a little technique practice. No football player would dream of a warmup which consisted only of short sprints and which didn't include the skills of his position: catching the ball, kicking, or tackling. Yet many time trialists warm up by pounding down the road and ignore the start and the turnaround, specific techniques whose sloppy execution could cost a lot of valuable time.

Casebeer is an exception and he recommends you practice starts and turnarounds at speed. Go to the actual starting line and try a few starts in the gear you'll use to be sure it doesn't skip when you stomp on it hard. If possible practice a few turnarounds at the actual location of the turn on the course at speeds approximating race speeds. Look for the limits before the race, not during it.

I covered the pros and cons of motorpacing in an earlier chapter. Quite a few riders see it as essential before a time trial. Hammer says he motorpaces for 15 to 20 minutes before the start in 53x15 and 16. The 7-Eleven team took the first four places in the individual TT at the 1983 Pan Am trials and Phinney reports that "20 miles of our warmup was motorpacing at high speed behind a van." But of course there is a catch. "Great for warming up," Phinney adds, "but very dangerous." Before you decide to use a motorpaced warm up be sure you are a good bike handler and that you have an experienced driver.

How much time should you allow between the end of your warmup and the start? "A few seconds," says Twigg. "Roll around easy for five minutes until the start," says Resh. This is one that you'll have to work out for yourself on the basis of your own experience.

Some riders like to be a little late so they are rolling up to the line as their minute man vanishes down the road, their coach or supporters are yelling in alarm, and everyone thinks they'll miss their start. They proclaim that this sense of urgency gives them an extra shot of adrenaline. Other riders like several minutes at the start to breathe deeply, compose their thoughts, and concentrate on the event to come.

15
The start

Nervous? It's normal,
but you need to control it

WHEN YOUR WARMUP is finished, shift into the right gear for the starting conditions at the race. Choose a gear in advance that is low enough so you can get it turning without struggling too much. It should be high enough so you don't reach an inefficiently high cadence too early and have to waste time with needless shifts.

As I mentioned earlier, try a couple of starts at the actual starting line so you are ready for gentle grades that may alter your choice of gear. Unless the start is immediately and steeply uphill, start in the big ring since shifts are easier to make on the rear than on the front. That way you won't be in danger of throwing your chain due to shifts that you force in the excitement.

Your strength at the start will determine what gear you actually use. Remember that you'll be pulling on the bars for all you are worth so upper-body strength has a lot to do with how high a gear you can use. A big, muscular rider like Potoff often uses a 53x14. He says he "likes to use every muscle in my upper body and really muscle the bike until I can get it cranking."

Most riders use the next-to-the-largest freewheel sprocket: usually a 17 on a straight block. As in normal riding, never use the largest cog because the resulting chain line is quite inefficient and it is easy to have the chain skip.

Be sure the chain is dead center on the freewheel cog you've chosen. Pedal a few revolutions backwards and then try an all-out start to be sure. Sometimes everything will seem okay with a cursory inspection in the excitement right before the start. But when you rip away from the line the chain will skip or even autoshift, a situation guaranteed to destroy your concentration and maybe even cause a crash.

Start your watch when the rider ahead of you, your minute man, takes off. That way you'll have an accurate record of your time by just subtracting a minute from what appears on the watch. Occasionally timers inadvertently stop their watches before everyone finishes so keep your own time as a backup. If the course is marked off by the mile you can figure out your splits too.

After your minute man is gone, roll up to the line and be sure one foot is in the pedal and the strap snugged down. Then, with the holder supporting your bike, get the other foot in. Don't tighten the toe straps too much or your feet will get numb later in the ride. However, the start is like a sprint. If you're trying to get a fairly big gear rolling from a dead stop and there is too much play, you are apt to pull a foot out of the pedal 10 feet from the line and land on your head. The spectators will laugh, you'll be embarrassed, and you'll lose some time. Of course, if you use the new strapless pedals you'll be spared all these agonies.

Position your crankarm for maximum power. Potoff says, "I always position my right foot about 10 o'clock so when I'm finally let go I can really come out hard."

Paulin suggests you "breathe harder than you think necessary at the start so you don't go into oxygen debt." Don't overdo it though. Physiologists say that shallow, rapid breathing doesn't help and that any extra oxygen you suck into your lungs before the race has no benefit once you begin. And deep breathing can make you lightheaded. Still, it has a relaxing, therapeutic effect for some riders. You may be nervous enough that a few deep breaths will help calm the butterflies that are doing barrel rolls in your stomach.

It is normal to be nervous before the race. If you aren't, you are probably flat and stale for the event. Pre-race jitters are a sign that your mind and body are ready for maximum effort. Some riders get so worked up that they can't keep food down. For most people it is a queasy sensation in the stomach coupled with leaden legs.

Butterflies? For me it is more like a Lear jet, but some riders report DC-10s or space shuttles. In any case, welcome the feeling in the period of time an hour or so before the start. It means all systems are operating and ready. If you feel that way the night before, it is too early. By the time the event begins your sharp mental edge may be dulled.

Good riders have learned to control their nervousness, turning it on shortly before a race when it is most advantageous but thinking about other things when too much adrenaline would be premature. More on this subject in the chapter on psychology.

After your minute man leaves, the starter will tell you how much time you have left and start a countdown at five or 10 seconds to go. Stand up on the pedals with about five seconds to go. Some riders rock forward slightly in time with the countdown. When the starter says "Go!" they can explode forward with their body weight and get a little momentum behind the first pedal stroke.

How strong a start?

The intensity of your start is a subject of controversy. Some riders swear by a foot-stomping blast away from the line, nostrils flaring and eyes popping with a primal scream thrown in for effect. They argue that you have so much adrenaline built up that it is good to let it all out at the start – something like the way the first hit in a football game releases the pre-game nervousness. Others prefer to finesse the start and save that energy to apportion out over the whole race.

The arguments for the latter method are pretty impressive. Phinney says that starting should be "fairly relaxed, depending on the length of the time trial. Too many riders make the mistake of starting too fast and going anaerobic which requires slowing down to recover." Shumway agrees: "I avoid becoming anaerobic at the start. It is better to constantly build up speed and stay there than start out too hard and have to slow down."

Hammer reports: "I had an opportunity to observe some pros in Europe this summer and was impressed by their smoothness and concentration when starting." Brandt cautions: "Don't come out smoking! If you hammer off the start line, you risk hyperventilating and waste time recovering. Start with a strong, steady acceleration the first three or four minutes and then increase your effort to maximum steady state."

Olavarri says, "It is important to get off to a strong start but not too strong. I've started too fast before – like a pursuit start – and found myself totally blown in the first mile. It took me two more miles to recover. Needless to say, this was not one of my better performances." Kiefel concludes, "Don't rocket off the line and blow up in less than a mile."

This view isn't the last word though. Remember that appearances can be deceiving. Many top riders use a big gear and get 200 yards down the road in a hurry but they don't look very fast. They keep their elbows in, they accelerate smoothly, and they ride a straight line but they are going faster than many less adept cyclists whose flailing styles merely waste energy.

Some riders find that deep breathing helps them feel more calm in the moments before the start. Pre-race jitters are normal and are a sign that your mind and body are ready for maximum effort.

The length of the time trial is a factor too. Twigg cautions that "the shorter the event, the more important the start. You have to start fairly fast so you don't lose too much time." And Casebeer is even more emphatic: "If you start too slowly you'll probably keep that speed the whole time." Know yourself. If you practice starts like I suggested in the training section, you'll know exactly what works best for you.

And don't discount the effects of emotion. Though she's usually calm and rational, Twigg's eyes flash a little when she thinks of the start of a time trial. "I'm usually pretty psyched up," she says. "It is a sprint."

So maybe cyclists worry too much about saving energy at the start. Maybe we would be better off to get a little wild-eyed before a time trial and ride more aggressively. Cycling has a reputation as a thinker's sport, one that rewards calculation and pacing, penalizing those who ride emotionally without regard for the painful consequences of anaereobic effort. But adrenaline is a powerful stimulant and athletes in other sports have discovered that they can exceed what they perceived as their limits if they get the emotions and the body working together. Experiment.

After the start, pedal up that first gear to a high cadence while standing up, then get back in the saddle. Shift to the next gear only when your cadence is about 10 r.p.m. higher than the cadence you hope to maintain in your primary gear for most of the race. If you are pedaling slowly and shift to a bigger gear, you'll get bogged down. It will be difficult to get your cadence up without standing again, a practice that wastes energy and is inefficient because of the large surface you present to the wind. "I don't shift until I have leg speed," says Twigg. And Olavarri sums up: "I'm better off to start in a 53x16, get my momentum going, catch my breath, shift into the 14, and keep going."

16
Cadence and gearing

Maintain your optimum r.p.m.
in the highest gear you can

TWO SCHOOLS of thought dominate discussions of the most efficient cadence for a time trial. One theory is to use the biggest gear possible and let your cadence settle at whatever rate your legs can handle in that gear. The other view is that a low cadence is inefficient and slow and that you should avoid a gear so large that your cadence drops below about 90 rpm. Despite appearances, there really isn't an argument here. Both groups are doing what is natural and feels good for them based on long years of experience.

For instance, Phinney says, "Individual time trialing for me comes down to the biggest gear I can use (efficiently), the faster the time. I can't maintain a high r.p.m. like I would in a team time trial so I generally use a big gear: 53x13 or 12."

It is important to consider two qualifiers here. First is Davis' parenthetical note: efficiently. He is not using a 53x12 so he can brag about it after the race. Many riders do this but your gearing isn't recorded in the results — only your time. Davis is using it because it feels good and his experience tells him that is what will get him the fastest time.

Also, when Davis says that he can't maintain as fast a cadence as in a team time trial, that doesn't mean he is pedaling slowly. His cadence is only slower in relative terms. For instance, in 1981 Davis rode a 55:41 in the district championships in terrible conditions that featured a 30 m.p.h. headwind on the return leg. So if he rode a 53x13 he still averaged an r.p.m. of about 85. That is fairly slow but it isn't the kind of leg-deadening plod that so many inexperienced riders assume is necessary in time trials.

Olavarri used about the same cadence to set her American women's record of 57:37 in a gear of 53x14. A lot of strong time trialers would like to break 58 minutes but they think they need a 53x12 to do it. Not so.

Potoff chooses higher gearing and somewhat lower cadence because of his experience. "I'm able to ride a 108- or 109-inch gear [52x13] somewhere between 80 and 90 r.p.m. This is just a style that I've worked with over the years and it has worked well." Casebeer comments, "Some people are stompers so for them lower r.p.m. may be better."

Roy Knickman is at the other end of the spectrum. "I've always been more of high-cadence person," he reports. "I've ridden national championship time trials with the Junior gear limit and only used the biggest gear half the time. I'd use 53x16. I like to keep 100 r.p.m. and have a rhythm so I'm really moving. I rode a TT once when I was just back from the worlds. No special TT wheels or anything. The course record was 21:56 (10 miles) and everyone praised that as the world's best. I used a 14 or 15 the whole way but kept my r.p.m. up and it worked – I rode a 21:22. No matter how bad I was hurting I kept it about 100 to 102. That seems to be where I pedal."

Kiefel agrees. "I start out in a high cadence and then try to keep my leg speed at 95 r.p.m. If I can spin my 53x14 rather than slog along in a 13 or 12, I go that much faster." Casebeer points out: "Look at Junior times – 55 to 57 minutes for the best 25-miler with a 52x15. So you don't need to have big gears to go fast."

Twigg is even more emphatic, arguing that "the key to being a good time trialist is keeping your cadence up. It is more important to have a fast cadence than to pound bigger gears and go slower and slower. I did some really fast time trials when I was limited to Junior gears. You don't need gears that big." Part of Twigg's preference for higher r.p.m. time trialing may stem from her experience riding on the track where the fixed gear requires a supple, fast spin.

What this shows is that cadence is a highly individual thing. Your cycling background, temperament, and physiological makeup will dictate your most efficient rate. However, nearly everyone agrees that it will be found somewhere in the range between 80 and 100 r.p.m. Remember that at a cadence of 100 you'll be going a little over 25 m.p.h. in a modest 53x17, a pace that will get you under the hour for 25 miles.

Even the most macho of the big-gear grinders cautions that if you drop below 80, you're dead. Once your cadence falls to the point where you are laboring in a gear too large for your fitness and the conditions you'll never get your cadence or your speed up again.

I found out the truth of that at the national championships in

1981 at Bear Mountain, New York. The time trial course was not
the usual flat route but had several substantial climbs. I tried to
muscle over them in 53x17 and my muscle wasn't up to the task.
I found myself standing up and plodding painfully in terminal oxygen debt long before the top. When I got to flatter ground, I couldn't
get my cadence back up to 95-100 no matter how low a gear I used.
My legs felt dead. My brain kept telling them to speed up and my
quads kept yelling back "Forget it!"

As a result I rode badly. If I'd spun up the hills in a lower gear
I would have lost little if any time and still been able to pedal fast
on the flats. I knew all that before the race began but it is easy in
the heat of competition to equate speed with gearing rather than
cadence and not shift down.

If you are inexperienced what cadence should you try to shoot for
until you establish your own best r.p.m.? What is the optimum cadence for most riders? Eddie B says that a cadence between 86-92
is the proper range for time trialing.

Research on cadence

A recent scientific study by an exercise physiologist reinforces
what athletes and coaches have known for years from experience —
that a cadence of about 90 r.p.m. is the most efficient pedaling rate
for the average trained cyclist. A number of earlier studies had indicated that rates as low as 50-60 r.p.m. were the most efficient. But
these studies were done on recreational cyclists who were not accustomed to higher cadences. Also, the subjects were tested on ergometers, where it is nearly impossible to establish a racing position.

To remedy these flaws in the early investigations, Jim Hagberg
at Washington University in St. Louis designed a new study. He
used highly trained, competitive cyclists riding their own bikes on
a treadmill.

The results showed that riders were most efficient (as indicated
by lower heart rate, oxygen consumption, ventilation, blood lactate,
and perceived exertion) at an average pedaling rate of 91 r.p.m.

Now that coaches and researchers finally agree on the most efficient cadence, the question is why it should be so. Explains Hagberg: "The real advantage may be that the same total work required
during each minute is peformed in smaller, more manageable units
when pedaling faster."

But if your cadence settles naturally at 85 or 98 instead of 91 you

Greg LeMond uses a bicycle computer to monitor his progress in this 11-mile time trial stage of the '85 Coors Classic. Note that he keeps an aerodynamic position despite the effort of maintaining his optimum cadence in a big gear.

don't necesarily get more efficient if you change it. Although 91 was the average optimum rate for the seven riders in the study, the most efficient cadence for individual riders varied from 72 to 103 r.p.m. This means that 91 isn't gospel but leaves plenty of room for personal variation in riding style, muscle fiber make-up, and biomechanical factors like length of the femur.

So, while scientific studies like this one are interesting and revealing, what they reveal most is that we are each unique and we need to listen to our own bodies to determine what is optimum for us. Science can't give us some miracle number that will make us world beaters. That is good because a large part of the fascination of cycling is in finding out just how our bodies work. Train within the range of cadence that the study suggests and have fun looking for the rate that works best for you.

Measuring cadence

So our original question – how do you select a gear for a time trial? – is the wrong question. You really don't select a gear for a time trial. Instead, you find your optimum cadence and then use progressively higher gears until you can just barely keep that cadence for the length of the race.

How do you know what cadence you are pedaling? One way is to count pedal revolutions for 15 seconds and multiply by four (or for 10 seconds times six). Count each time your right foot hits bottom. If you wear your watch on your wrist, instead of strapped to the bars, turn the face to the inside where you take your pulse. With your hands on the drops in the time trialing position you can see the watch by merely rolling your wrist upward slightly.

A more precise method is to use one of the bicycle computers like a Pacer, Push, or CycleCoach. These register your cadence exactly, so you can be assured you are cranking out the precise number of r.p.m. that experience in training and racing has shown is best for you.

I'd like to see a manufacturer come out with a very small light-weight unit, aerodynamically shaped, that recorded only cadence. This would require a single wire running from the sensor on the cranks, up behind the seat tube, and along the top tube with the rear brake cable. The monitor could be shielded behind the handlebars instead of mounted on top. The result would be a very clean unit both aerodynamically and aesthetically, unlike some units now being sold that give you loads of information, mostly useless, but are bulky, unsightly, and present a large surface to the air.

Position and pacing

When you have settled into your optimum cadence, focus for a moment on your position. You have worked on your aerodynamic riding profile in training. Don't let the excitement of competition cause you to forget it, sit up, and catch more air with your upper body than you need to. Keep your back almost flat, your head up, and don't let your elbows stick out in the wind.

It is not hard to maintain a good position when you are practicing it in training in a 42x17. But in a race when you are on the ragged edge of blowing up it is tempting to flail all over the bike in the mistaken notion that you'll go faster. Even as experienced a time trialer as Olavarri says, "I am conscious of my position always. Even in the start I try to keep my head lower and my hips up."

Knickman says it too. "With time trialing it is just being as steady as possible, as efficient as possible − no body movement − just down the road."

Your pacing is critical. Only experience will teach you how hard you can go in the first half of the race and still be able to keep your speed up to the end. I have seen riders who blast away from the line and do the first several miles at 28 m.p.h. when their best 25 is 1:02 or 1:03. Then they blow up completely and do three-quarters of the race at 23 m.p.h. in a 53x12 at 65 or 70 r.p.m. This is a tempting trap to fall into. Use your bike computer, your watch, or your experience to set a steady pace that you can maintain to the end. Then if you have something left over, pick up the pace in the last third of the race.

This is easy to say but the trick involves knowing just how fast you can go the whole distance. It is almost always faster than you think if you go steadily. Or, put another way, you can hurt more than you think you can. Knickman exaggerates only a little when he says, "If you hit the turnaround and don't think you're dead yet, you're not going fast enough."

Of course being steady is the secret. If you get panicked five miles out and try to pick up the pace too rapidly you'll go into oxygen debt. Instead, increase your cadence several revolutions per minute and see how it goes, giving your body time to adjust to the new level of exertion. Remember, you are looking for your anaerobic threshold, the very edge of your steady state. If you go over it you'll pay a heavy price in a slowed pace down the road. "You only win if you are regular and steady, your body like a clock," says Eddie B.

Once you get rolling, there are a couple of tricks that may help your time trialing. One is a method of breathing that keeps your mouth from going dry and aids free air passage. In his book *Bicycle Road Racing*, Eddie B suggests that you breathe during a time trial with your lower jaw jutted slightly out and the tip of your tongue resting behind your lower front teeth. Try this in your hard training and notice how you get more saliva flow as well as unobstructed breathing.

Olavarri has another suggestion on breathing: "I think about my breathing during time trials. By concentrating more on the exhalation and simply allowing the inhalation to happen (not forcing a breath in) I can relax more, particularly in the upper body."

Eddie's other suggestion sounds, frankly, ridiculous but he guarantees that it works. He suggests that you rest one leg at a time by soft-pedaling for one revolution out of every five or six with one leg, then five revolutions later repeat the process with the other leg. He claims that your speed will increase because each leg will do about 10% less work throughout the race and thus will be able to generate more force when it is pedaling hard.

The drawback of this method is that it takes a lot of practice before the race and concentration during it to feel comfortable. If you can't get the rhythm of alternately easing off on one leg every six strokes, try soft-pedaling with both legs one revolution out of every 10.

Sound interesting? Some riders dismiss the technique as useless, a few swear by it, and others have never heard of it. You might want to experiment in training while you are doing repeats and compare your times with Eddie's technique to your standard style.

17
Concentration
*Don't let traffic and passing riders
interrupt your rhythm*

YOU STARTED well, your position is good, you're in a gear that
allows you to keep your cadence at your optimum level, you are
working hard but feel strong and steady. Now is the time to focus
your mind on keeping your speed at the highest levels possible.
You've practiced this in training but even so it is incredibly easy
to let your mind wander to something more pleasant than the pain
you are experiencing.

There is no escaping the fact that riding at your maximum level
of sustainable speed — your anaerobic threshold — is a painful experience. Taking a cue from the tachometer in a sports car, time trialists call it "red lining." You are riding at an intensity just below
the level where your body could no longer handle the waste products of muscle function and you would go into oxygen debt. Go just
a little faster and you blow your engine. As Steve Woznick, a bronze
medalist in the 1,000-meter time trial at the 1975 Pam Am Games,
said, "You've got to be willing to rip it all apart, even yourself."

Not every rider can do it. Just as there is physical talent involved
that is genetically predetermined and thus essentially out of your
control, so ability to either block out or overcome this pain is beyond
the capacity of some riders. That is one reason why some excellent
road riders are atrocious time trialers.

Knickman describes a top road racer and a member of the national team who "was strong enough to climb well with a lot of
power in the national championships and stage racing but when it
came to time trialing he couldn't get out of his own way." There are
people who just don't seem to have it mentally.

It takes practice to learn how to push yourself to that intensity.
If your concentration drops off just a little, your speed will slacken
because your body is smarter than you are. It doesn't want to hurt
this much and it dislikes the kind of physiological brinksmanship

that anaerobic threshold riding entails. But if you don't ride with
your physiological tachometer on the red line, accompanied by all
the feelings of discomfort that such a level of exertion implies, you
won't be going as fast as you could. There is no shortcut, no easy
way out. "Only pain guarantees success," says Eddie B.

East Germany has produced some of the world's best time trialists
in the last few years. Coaches from that country know the importance of the mental control that opens the door to these performance
levels. The East German national coach, in an interview at the 1983
Coors Classsic, made the point emphatically. "The best racers are
the best at concentrating on the event."

Concentration doesn't necessarily mean a beady-eyed and trance-
like mental fixation on your spinning feet or your labored breathing. As I'll explain in another chapter, even the best endurance athletes, the most ferocious focusers on their event, disassociate at times.
Hearing music in their heads is one way top riders get a little edge.
Twigg comments that "concentration for a sustained period of time
is a key element in time trialing. Sometimes I have a song going
in my head but it doesn't mean that I'm not concentrating. It is just
to keep my rhythm going. I don't have any favorites, just whatever
happens to pop into my head."

Since time trialing is a steady rhythmical event, mental music
with a strong background beat works best. Try out different songs
in training until you find one that works, then listen to it half a
dozen times just as you wake up on the morning of the race. This
seems to fix the beat in your head. If you've ever had an alarm clock
that wakes you to music, then gone nearly berserk as that initial
song danced through your head all morning, you know what I mean.

I don't recommend time trialing to actual music using a portable
cassette player. You need to be able to mentally turn those tunes
on and off in a race as the need arises. Fumbling with the buttons
on a Walkman won't help your concentration. Quite a few riders
train, headphones firmly in place, tooling down the road with their
tunes blaring in their ears. I wonder how safe this is. It seems to
me that it would be difficult to hear approaching traffic. It is also
illegal in some states.

Don't forget to watch where you are going in your ferocious concentration. Sight is safety too. Time trialing is a safer event than
road racing in one respect − there aren't 30 other riders right there
with you − but can be incredibly dangerous if you aren't alert. In
the 1983 season there were reportedly six fatalities in England in

Cars and contestants can be a real test of your concentration, as in this 4.7-mile uphill time trial in Kentucky.

time trial events. You are reponsible for your own safety. You can't trust course marshalls, drivers, officials, or other riders. So wear a good helmet, keep your head up, and, instead of riding at 100% of your capacity, ride at 99.5% and employ that extra half percent for the task of getting you safely to the finish.

Keeping your head up has another function besides safety, as Knickman found out. "I never used to be able to ride a really straight line. I'd kind of move a little bit. I was riding pursuit and my coach said, 'You're looking down at your front wheel. You look like a turtle.' But when I looked up I could automatically ride a straight line. And it straightened up my back which helped my position."

Although it seems self-evident, a straight line will get you there faster. In the heat of competition many riders forget and add yards to the distance they have to go by moving around in the lane when the road is straight. Usually the best place to ride is the two-foot strip where the right wheels of cars travel. This area will be smoother than the pavement nearer the edge of the road because of the flattening effect of the traffic. For the same reason it is also more likely to be clearer of debris. You are far enough to the right to allow cars to pass safely yet not so far over that you have little margin for error on your right.

Always ride at least a foot or so from the right side of the road so you have some room to maneuver. The law in most states says that cyclists must ride as far to the right as is practicable. This doesn't mean as far right as is possible, it means as far as is safe. Even in the excitement of a time trial, you have to insist on your fair share of the road.

Passing

Many experienced competitors try to speed up slightly when they pass another rider. Time trials are primarily races against yourself, but the competitive instinct is always there. I confess that the sight of my minute man ahead, getting closer and closer, gives me a little more drive even when I think I am going as fast as I can. So if you are competitive by nature, use your minute man as a goal to shoot for. Riders with more experience in road racing or some other competitive sport find that concentrating on the people ahead of them is the most effective way to go faster. The riders ahead provide external motivation. As Twigg explains, "I think it is a psychological uplift to pass someone."

Some riders make a game out of this aspect of the race. Paulin reports, "I love to blow by my minute or two-minute man." Casebeer says he plays leapfrog: "I try to catch people. My record is 28 in a 25-miler."

You do have to be careful not to get into oxygen debt if you speed up to pass someone. As Potoff explains, "Since I'm riding on the ultimate edge of my ability, it wouldn't take that much to go into oxygen debt if I did something foolish like really flying by. I make that rider chase me, not the other way around."

Traffic

A potential distraction you'll have to contend with on most courses is vehicular traffic. Its presence underscores the need for caution and heads-up riding, literally and figuratively. Most drivers are courteous and will give you a wide berth, especially if the race promoter has prominent signs posted warning drivers that a race is in progress. However, just as you encounter unpleasant folks while training, you can expect a few bad actors while you are racing too.

One year at a USCF district time trial a local resident, angered at the use of what he obviously considered to be his personal road, cruised back and forth on the course passing riders too closely and then slowing abruptly in front of them. Luckily no accidents took place. The state patrol cited the motorist for careless driving but quite a few riders complained that their concentration had been ruined for the rest of the race. This is a poor attitude, a loser's attitude. For all they knew, other riders in contention had been subjected to the same distractions and so they were on even terms. Or the motorist may not have cost them as much time as it seemed in the emotions surrounding the incident.

In such cases push on through to the end as if nothing had happened, since you never know the fate of the other competitor. Consider the errant driver as just one more road hazard like glass or potholes. Be observant, avoid the offending car as you would any obstruction, and continue your best effort without letting negative thoughts disrupt your focus on going fast.

It is tempting to make obscene gestures, think about just what you would do if you could get hold of the driver, or philosophize about the sorry state of human nature in general. Save your wish-fulfillment fantasies or profound speculations for after the race. By that time maybe the miscreant will have been caught.

Complaining to yourself about driver harassment is no more beneficial than complaining about objective dangers like normal road hazards over which we have no control. It is like basketball players and coaches who complain about the officiating. In both cases it takes away from concentration on the event and provides a handy excuse for poor performance.

It is tempting in the effort and pain of a time trial to use bad pavement, fickle winds, or the actions of a small minority of drivers as reasons to slow down, excuses to ease off just a little or bag the event entirely. Winners do their best in the face of adversity and then patiently await the posting of the results, knowing that they couldn't have gone any faster under the circumstances. Here endeth the sermon.

Cars and trucks aren't all negative. Passing vehicles can help you to a faster time. I am told that one reason the British post such great times is because they often hold big events on four-lane highways jammed with high-speed traffic. The passing vehicles create a kind of continuous draft, upping average speeds a mile or more per hour. One disgruntled American official, noting the phenomenal British times, was heard to remark that the next step was to hold time trials on busy airport runways and get a draft from DC-10s.

In contrast, most U.S. time trials are held on relatively isolated roads. But alert riders use whatever passing traffic is available. When a car or better yet a large truck goes by, accelerate slightly to take advantage of the draft. A small car is worth two or three r.p.m. for 50 yards. An 18-wheeler might give you 10 r.p.m. for a quarter mile depending on how close it comes to your elbow.

There is nothing illegal about this. It isn't drafting in a technical sense, since the passing traffic is going at least twice as fast as you are. Yet many riders don't know how to use this advantage, giving their opponents an edge. Nor is this technique unethical since every rider has the opportunity to benefit equally, given equal volumes of traffic during an event.

Any help you get from vehicles going your way is nearly negated by the wall of air blasting you from oncoming cars. They'll be farther away from you so the effect isn't as great. But when the twin brother of that 18-wheeler that helped when he passed you comes blasting back in the opposite direction, it sometimes feels like you've hit the invisible energy shield of science fiction.

The correct procedure in the face of that blast is the same as for overtaking vehicles. Pick up your r.p.m. a little so that, when the moving wall of air hits, you won't lose momentum and have your cadence drop below your optimum race rate. If it does, it is hard to get it back up again. At least until another truck flies by going your way.

18
Wind and hills

Here's your chance to gain time
over less determined competitors

MOST TIME TRIALISTS hate wind because they ride time trials to post a good time and a strong wind often robs them of that opportunity. Headwinds are unpleasant to ride into because you are working so hard, going much slower than normal, yet there is no visible obstacle. The road stretches out flat before you but it feels like you are dragging a couple of cement blocks. At least you can see the grade of a hill but wind is the invisible enemy.

But most disadvantages can be turned to advantages if you view them properly. I doubt that Shakespeare rode any time trials, but when Hamlet says that "there is nothing either good or bad but thinking makes it so" he was demonstrating the correct mental attitude toward wind in competition or training. If your goal is to win, realize that you can gain more time on your competition in a headwind than in any other portion of the race.

For instance, if you normally train alone because there are few other riders in your area, you may view this forced solitary training as a disadvantage. But it can work in your favor too. Casebeer says: "Ride alone a lot and you won't notice the wind as much because you are always pushing the wind anyway."

Use power and position

One way to handle headwinds is to use your power. You may not have the leg speed to do well in high r.p.m. tailwind sections of the course but if you are extremely powerful you can muscle your way through headwinds that defeat other riders. Even for a powerful rider with good leg speed the headwind section is the best bet to gain time. It is tempting to think that you can use a big gear and spin past other riders in the tailwind but it doesn't work that way. Potoff explains: "Even with a reserve high gear to increase my speed substantially, the wind has increased everyone else's too. I'll take a calm day anytime."

Phinney says: "Headwinds I like, because weaker riders die and I just power through in the biggest gear possible." In the 1981 Colorado district championship time trial, the wind blew so hard on the treeless plains surrounding the course east of Colorado Springs that my car rocked from side to side as I sat in it before the race. But in conditions that found many riders four or five minutes slower than their best times, Davis won the event in 55:44.

Another powerful rider, three-time national TT champion Andy Weaver, often rides alone in the strong headwinds of his native state of Florida. "I like the wind," he enthuses. "I know I can gain time in the wind. It is a mental thing." So if you are a powerful rider, use the headwinds to your advantage.

What if you aren't? Training properly, of course, will help you develop the power you need. But any rider can take advantage of Eddie B's advice: "Fight wind with aerodynamic position and aerodynamic clothes."

In a headwind a tight skinsuit and a smooth helmet become even more important than in normal conditions. One-piece suits are fairly expensive but definitely worth the cost in seconds saved when wind would turn a road jersey into a sail. Be sure your number is attached so it doesn't flop in the wind. Many riders pin it on, then tape the edges down.

Some riders go so far as to put a broad strip of tape over their shoe laces and not wear gloves. I'm not sure how much these measures really help but they can't hurt. When you are battling into the teeth of the gale, you need all the help, physical and mental, that you can get.

The rule for gearing in a headwind is the same as in calm conditions: Keep your cadence up. Some riders have an attack of anxiety in headwinds if they even think about shifting down. As a result their cadence drops dramatically and with it their efficiency. The actual gear doesn't matter and will vary widely depending on the force of the wind. Use whatever you need to keep your cadence up and ignore the kind of self-defeating thoughts that equate overall speed solely with gearing.

Some headwinds are gusty and intermittent. In these conditions be alert for changes in your cadence and be ready to shift up or down in response to the capricious gusts. This can be incredibly frustrating. But the difficulty of maintaining optimum speed here means that if you can keep your cadence steady you'll gain even more time on less attentive competitors.

Crosswinds and tailwinds

Bad as headwinds can be, they are sometimes less of a problem than violent crosswinds. A strong gust of wind from the right side can blow you into the traffic lane abruptly where drivers passing you too close may not have time to react. From the left, the wind is always threatening to nudge you onto the bumpy shoulder of the road or clear into the gravel. You have to fight the bike to ride a straight line and this detracts from your concentration and ties up your arms, shoulders, and upper back sooner than they normally would become fatigued.

Some courses are exposed to the wind without any vegetation or buildings to block the onslaught. If the course has hedgerows or fields of corn next to it though, take advantage of this natural windbreak. If the wind is from the right, ride as close to the right side of the road as conditions will allow where you will get a little shelter from the storm.

Tailwinds can be trickier than inexperienced riders imagine. Casebeer says, "Go like hell," then adds, "but you must have enough left if you turn into the wind to make it back [to the start] at a smooth steady pace." If the tailwind is on the outward leg of the time trial follow Phinney's advice and use caution: "Hold something back."

I've seen riders in a moderate tailwind go all out in a big gear, their legs going like a hummingbird's wings, fooled by the sense of greater speed into thinking that they weren't working too hard. After the turn they had to fight the headwind and they soon found that there was nothing left. And remember that headwinds are where you can gain big chunks of time, not in tailwind conditions where another rider can go almost as fast yet expend substantially less energy.

Of course if the tailwind is on the homeward leg, give it all you have left. Hammer advises you to "use the highest gear possible, maintain good body position, keep riding at the anaerobic threshold. It is easy to slack off when the going gets easy. Consequently I try to keep working very hard." Mereness, after winning the Colorado district TT in 30 m.p.h. winds, said, "I was breathing harder with the tailwind than with the headwind." Experienced riders like Mereness and Hammer know how to turn the apparent disadvantages of wind to their favor.

How to ride hills

Not all time trial courses are flat. American time trialing developed from the British model where flat, fast courses were sought out because times were important in national rankings. A hilly course in one part of the country would penalize that area's riders. European time trials, on the other hand, tend to be more like road race courses. There are plenty of hills with some tight corners thrown in.

As I mentioned, the course used for the 1981 nationals at Bear Mountain was a departure from the usual flat course used for the championships. This was due to available terrain rather than conscious planning but it produced some vehement reactions. Riders from Colorado called the course "rolling." Riders from flatter states called it "mountainous." I can't repeat what others called it.

Interestingly enough, the hills didn't change the relative order of the top riders very much compared to previous years and flatter courses. Tom Doughty had set the national record of 52:25.9 on a flat course in Bisbee, Arizona, in 1980. Many onlookers didn't expect him to do well in the hills because he was a big powerful rider not noted as a climber. Yet he successfully defended his national title with a 56:33, more than half a minute ahead of his nearest rival.

On a sustained climb, like the 28-mile Mount Evans Hillclimb, small, light-framed riders have an advantage. But flat time trial power converts readily to handle the shorter hills on the usual time trial course.

There are a few tricks, though. You may have noticed that times on hilly courses aren't generally that much slower than on the flat. This often fools even experienced riders. Quite a few people predicted that no one would break the hour on the Bear Mountain course. Yet Doughty's time was three and a half minutes faster than that.

Casebeer, who was fourth on that same course, observes, "Up the hill it slows you down but down the hill you are twice as fast." So don't think of riding only to the top of the hill. Concentrate on riding over it so you'll have the energy to take advantage of gravity on the downhill to make up some of the time lost on the way up.

Another trick, recommended by Resh, is to ride the course beforehand if it is hilly so you will know what gears to use. Some hills are straightforward. One shift will get you over the top. Others are staircased, terraced affairs that require a subtle sense of gradient to keep your cadence up. The worst are abrupt walls that require one or more shifts part way up. A blown shift can destroy not only

If a hill is too long to sprint over, you should gear down to keep your cadence and momentum up.

your cadence but your forward momentum as well. So check out hilly courses to know what you are in for.

In the saddle or out?

On short hills (100 to 200 meters) the general rule still applies: Keep your cadence up. But it is worth venturing slightly over the anaerobic threshold to maintain your speed without wasting the time needed to shift once before the hill and once after. You are in less danger of blowing up because you can recover slightly on the downhill even if you make a mistake and extend yourself too far. You won't gain any time going downhill if you blow up slightly at the crest of the hill but you won't lose much either. And if you have done intervals as part of your regular training you will have the ability to recover from anaerobic effort.

So on short shallow hills, says Hammer, who won the age 35-40 title at Bear Mountain, "Attack hard, maintaining the same gear and cadence as long as possible." Eddie B recommends that you stand up on short, steep hills.

Twigg grimaces. "I hate hills in the time trials because they break your cadence. On little rollers I stand up near the top unless I'm really hurting my legs. If it is something really steep I'll gear down instead of standing up."

Phinney succinctly sums up: "I try to power over without blowing up."

Longer hills require a different approach. You don't want to stand and grunt up a mile-long hill, wasting energy and having your cadence slow. Remember that the only reason to stand on short hills is to keep your cadence up in the same gear you used on the flat. If the hill is too long to sprint over in this fashion, Eddie B advises you to "stay seated, shift down, and move to the back of the saddle to push over. You must use your derailleur in a time trial."

Maybe you have noticed in road races or group training rides that when you come to a long hill some riders will stand up and climb rhythmically in a fairly large gear. But if you use a gear maybe a tooth or two lower you can stay seated and spin along beside them, using less energy.

In a group this effect is more pronounced because you have other riders around to gauge your speed. By yourself in a time trial you are likely to feel faster standing because you are working harder and using a bigger gear. Don't make this mistake. "The worst thing you can do on a hill," says Resh, "is ride in too big a gear." It will slow your cadence, destroy your legs, and hurt so much that any aggressive feelings you've managed to sustain through the pain you've encountered thus far will be washed away in a sea of lactic acid. On hills, on flats, in winds of all kinds – keep your cadence up!

Many riders alternate sitting and standing on longer climbs to work the muscles in different ways. Use a gear one or two teeth higher when you stand and slow your cadence slightly. You'll have to experiment to see how this technique works for you. Quite a few good climbers stay in the saddle most of the time. They claim that standing is inefficient over the long haul because their aching legs have the additional task of supporting their body weight.

The tough part, of course, is the post-race evaluation of what you did on the hill. Without other riders near you to gauge your progress it is difficult to tell if you were faster in a certain gear-cadence combination than in another. Even experienced time trialists find it hard to know.

In the Niwot time trial stage of the 1983 Coors Classic, Weaver finished fifth, two seconds out of third and only nine seconds away from the winner. He pushed the early hill in 54x17 seated all the way. When he reached the top he shifted immediately to the 12.

About two miles further on he hit a little hill, just a roller, and blew up. He had to go to the 13 to keep it rolling while he recovered.

Looking at those nine ticks of the clock that separated him from first place, Andy second-guessed himself after the race. What would have happened had he used a smaller gear on the hill and a 13 over the top, thus saving enough to use the 12 on the relatively flat run-in to the finish? "What you don't know," he mused, "is if that would have made me faster. The way it was, I felt awful but maybe I was going as fast as I could."

The hillclimb time trial

Some time trials are uphill all the way. There's the one in Colorado that I've mentioned – the Bob Cook Memorial Mt. Evans Hillclimb – that gains about 7,000 vertical feet in 28 miles and tops out on the summit at over 14,000 feet. Mt. Evans isn't a time trial in the true sense of the phrase because it is a mass-start event. However, the pack usually stays together only for the relatively shallow climbing of the first five miles, then spreads out dramatically. So for most riders it is an individual effort. The grade isn't at all severe but the distance wears down even well-trained riders who aren't mentally prepared for what it takes. One year, I remember, the New Zealand national team was spread out all over the climb in various stages of exhaustion.

Prepare for hillclimbs by riding a lot of long hills. There is really no substitute for the prolonged pushing and sustained effort of big climbs. If you are aiming for a hillclimb time trial, do long steady climbs instead of intervals at least once a week for a month before the event.

There is no real trick to this sort of race. Powerful but lightweight riders have an advantage, especially if they have the concentration to time trial well on the flat. Find out in advance what gears are necessary either by riding the course or by talking to other riders you trust.

Wind on exposed stretches of high mountain climbs can make a substantial difference in gearing. On a switchbacked climb like Mt. Evans, you'll be in a 42x17 sailing up one part of the climb, then round a switchback to continue climbing the same grade with the wind in your face and have to struggle in a 42x21. Always have a reserve low gear so that if conditions are bad you have something to fall back on.

Longer cranks provide a little more leverage. Hammer reports that in Europe "longer cranks are used in very steep hillclimbs by leading climbers." This is also the reason that many mountain bikes come equipped with 180mm cranks.

A steady pace is important on long climbs. You have to climb at your own rate over the distance. Sharp surges may be great to discourage and drop other riders on climbs in road races. But in time trial conditions it is the clock you have to beat, not the guy panting along beside or behind you. With the negligible effects of drafting at slow climbing speeds the rider you surge on and drop now may steadily ride by you later.

So find a rhythm and a pace that you can maintain to the summit and stay with it. This is especially true at high elevation where even a short bit of hard effort can give you a new and deeper appreciation of the term "oxygen debt."

19
The turn
Since every second counts,
you should practice your technique

TO THE UNINITIATED, time trials might seem to be simple events requiring only a big motor but no technique or riding skills. But, as we have seen, varied and subtle skills are required to start efficiently, choose your appropriate individual cadence, tread on the dangerous edge of the anaerobic threshold, and maintain speed over hills and in tricky winds.

In traditional time trials the most important application of technique comes halfway through the race, at the turnaround. In one way the turnaround is easier than the corners in criteriums or road races – you don't have the confounding variables of riders surrounding you. But other factors make it at least as difficult. One is that you're coming up on a 180-degree turn at top speed. You rarely use your brakes for the 90-degree turns in a criterium or road race unless they are at the bottom of hills. But if you're approaching a 180-degree turn at 25 m.p.h. you need to time your braking actions precisely. Also, 180-degree turns require different technique compared to shallower, less acute-angled turns.

Add to this the fatigue factor. In a time trial you should be pushing for all you are worth right up to the turn cone, not, as in mass-start events, jockeying for position in the pack or freewheeling a little to slide into a convenient hole in the bunch. And fatigue of this magnitude can often blur the senses and blunt the judgment.

Finally, you can lose huge chunks of time and skin if you blow the turnaround. The worst case is trying to come through too fast and either crashing flat on the pavement or riding off the road, losing it on the soft, muddy shoulder and ending up smelling the flowers in the ditch. You can add at least a minute to your time in these circumstances as you clamber back on – more if you knocked your handlebars sideways, unshipped your chain, or bent a rim.

And if you banged your knee hard in the process, your efficiency will be severly hampered all the way to the finish.

For all these reasons, good turnaround technique is supremely important. The surprise is that so few riders practice it. Of all the top time trialists I talked to in preparing this book, only one or two report that they ever spend much time practicing turnarounds – or starts, for that matter. Most are road riders and feel that they get enough practice in the 200 or so corners of the average criterium to enable them to get around the one corner in a time trial.

But it isn't that simple. Turns of 180 degrees are rare in road racing and when they do appear, as in an out-and-back course, many riders handle them badly. Even a superb bike handler like Phinney emphasizes that "the turnaround is important, therefore practice is crucial. I pride myself on being very fast through the turn." So, regardless of your cycling background, practice that turn. It will save you time coming and going.

Try to check out the turnaround before the race. At shorter time trials, ride past during your warmup. If the event is so long that you won't ride the whole course beforehand, drive by on your way to the start. Twigg says to "look for gravel, how tight the turn is going to be." Some time trial promoters have signs telling riders that the turn is one mile or 200 meters ahead but many courses aren't marked officially.

The turn for the local 10-miler in Gunnison, Colorado, is marked with faded paint on the pavement. There are vague directions from the starter to "look for a ranch on the right." The first time I rode the event I went right on past and was headed for the West Elk Wilderness Area before I realized my mistake. So in the pre-race inspection choose a landmark that will remind you that the turn is imminent.

Some courses have nasty surprises. The turnaround at Bear Mountain had a short downhill beginning just around the corner from the cone. Unsuspecting riders shifted into a larger gear and increased speed only to abruptly come face to face with the cone and the wildly gesticulating marshall. They clamped on the brakes, skidded precariously through the turn, and then realized that they were in 53x12 to attack the former downhill that was now a minor mountain. Pre-race inspection of the course can spare you these misfortunes.

During the race maintain your speed right to the turn. Don't start to unconsciously ease off two miles down the road in anticipation of the respite, however brief, that the turn offers. "You have to keep that high speed the whole time," says Knickman. "If I hit the turnaround and I'm not ready to die, that means I'm not going hard enough." And Paulin says, "Go for the turnaround as if it were the finish, turn around, and do it again."

As you approach the cone and the turn marshall, still going as hard as you can, check behind you for cars coming up. The best way to do this is to look back under your left elbow, not over your shoulder. From your aerodynamic position on the drops, this technique involves only a minor shift of your head. You won't have to sit up, catching a lot of air, and twist your whole body. Check ahead of you too. If in doubt about the timing of an oncoming car with your turn, yield to the car. Better to lose a few seconds than to become a hood ornament.

Set up for the turn properly. You want to go through by yourself not near another rider, so you have the whole road to work with. Potoff thinks that as he nears the turnaround "one of the biggest mistakes I try to avoid is not reeling in the last rider who is just in front of me. I get rid of that rider. You want a clear shot at the turn."

Shift down about 50 yards from the cone or other corner mark so you'll be able to devote your full attention to the actual turn without fumbling for the shift lever. The correct gear depends on conditions. If you've had a headwind all the way and have been pounding away in, say, 53x17 you won't need to shift. That gear will be plenty low enough to let you accelerate away from the turn with the help of the tailwind without exerting the kind of energy you used at the start in the same gear. But in the opposite situation you might sail into the turn in 53x12 riding a small gale. In that case you'll need to shift into the lowest gear you can safely use with your large chainwheel, turn, accelerate back into the wind and assess the situation once you get rolling.

Approach the cone on the far right side of the road so that you have maximum road width to work with. The exception is if the edge of the road is littered with glass or small bits of gravel that could cause a puncture. This debris should be swept before the race but often this isn't done. Again the pre-race inspection will guide your actions.

Actual cornering technique is similar to cornering in any situation. Practice will tell you how long you can wait to brake and still get your speed down enough to get through the turn without falling

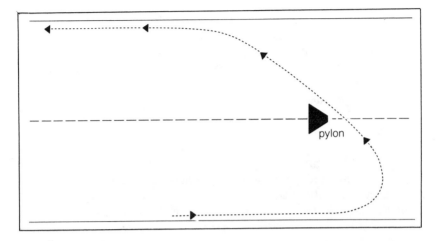

The 180-degree turn of the traditional out-and-back time trial takes practice. A shallow, lopsided arc is the best line to take because you will be able to pedal sooner.

or having the brakes lock and the tires skid just before the turn. Learn to cut this as close as possible. Potoff says, "Hit the brakes at the last possible second. Be real aggressive."

As you lean into the turn release the brakes, since laying the bike over with the brakes on can cause a skid. Put your outside pedal down, put your weight on it, and lean hard into the corner, nose over your left hand. Some riders stick out their left knee like a motorcyle road racer to help shift their weight into the turn. If the road is dry you'll be amazed at how much you can lean and still maintain traction, but only practice will demonstrate the limits.

Your line through the corner is crucial. As you can see from the diagram, your path through the corner shouldn't be a smooth curve with the cone in the middle but rather a bit lopsided. Go slightly past the cone and then lean it over hard so when you shave closely past the cone you are on a very shallow arc. This way you can start to pedal sooner since the bike is straightened up more and you won't catch a pedal.

Once around the cone get out of the saddle, sprint to a cadence faster than race pace as you did at the start, then sit down, shift, and really go after it. Here is the place to push at the very limits of your anaerobic threshold since you'll lose time if you don't regain your momentum quickly. If you've done your intervals in training and your recovery is good, you'll have some extra energy at this point because you coasted a little through the corner and recovered. The psychological uplift of knowing that you are on the way back helps too. So get mean, nasty, and aggressive. Blast out of that turn like you are sprinting for a Tour de France stage win.

20

The finish
and post-race

*Evaluation of your performance
can help you improve next time*

AFTER THE TURN you face the section of the race that is mentally
the most difficult. During the first half of a time trial you are relatively fresh and going hard to a clear and immediate objective – the
turnaround. The last quarter of the race is the time to push as hard
as you can with the finish line seemingly just down the road. But
that third quarter is brutal because you hurt so much and there is
still so far to go.

Even the best riders have this trouble. Kiefel confesses, "I almost
lost the 1983 nationals because I lost my concentration nine or 10
miles from the finish. Luckily I had enough left at the end to pull
it out." The long, lonely stretch from miles 13 to 20 has scuttled a
lot of potential PRs.

But out of adversity comes opportunity. This section of the race,
where many riders slack off a little, is your chance to gain time.
Everyone goes fast away from the line. A large percent of riders can
summon their reserves for a desperate finishing burst. But only if
you have excellent mental control and discipline can you go to the
limits in that no-man's land after the turnaround. That is the time
to summon all your emotional strength and tough it out. No guts,
no glory.

This is easy to say the night before the event or even five miles
into the race when you are cooking. But in the seemingly endless
stretch after the turn there aren't any technical tricks. Fancy equipment won't help, nor will techniques that you can practice in advance. It comes down to how close to your anaerobic threshold you
can ride, how much you are willing to put out to do well. At this
level of exertion, all pretenses get stripped away and you have to
take a look at your real self. You come up against the paradoxical

knowledge that although you know you could push harder, you can't.

Self-knowledge is a frightening thing because if you never seek your limits you can always fool yourself into believing that they are boundless. That is why time trials are such lonely events – what happens if you look deep inside and there is no one there? Some riders hate time trials simply because they hate this self-revelation. But limits are no reason for shame. Everyone has a breaking point and if you push hard enough you are sure to find yours. In time trials you'll find it quickly. That is no disgrace – the real shame is in being unwilling to look.

The finish

A strong finish in a time trial doesn't begin 500 or 1,000 meters from the line, but rather five miles or more away. If you save energy to squander all at once in a last-minute sprint you'll gain less time than if you used the same amount of energy to increase your speed less dramatically over a longer distance.

Knickman recalls: "Sometimes I'll test myself in smaller time trials to see if I have a sprint left. I remember we did some 10-mile time trials here [at the Olympic Training Camp]. I did a 20:59, which on a Junior gear was the fastest I'd ever gone. When I got near the line I tried to get out of the saddle and almost fell off the bike. You have to be able to judge yourself. With five seconds to go I could barely keep my eyes open I was hurting so bad. If you can sprint you haven't been going hard enough."

Save a little energy to keep your eyes open at the finish though. It is pretty congested there with riders coming across the line and timers and spectators milling around. Slow down gradually after you finish, keeping an eye out for road hazards.

Warmdown

After you finish, be sure to ride easily for at least 15 minutes to cool down. If you immediately jump off the bike and stand around talking, you are likely to be stiff and sore the next day. Five miles of gentle spinning helps you get composed and reduces your breathing to normal levels.

A well-conditioned rider recovers quickly after an all-out effort and his pulse rate may be at near-normal levels in just a few minutes. But real recovery takes longer and easy pedaling will allow you to start training hard again sooner after the event. It will also help reduce any potential injuries that are lurking in your ligaments and tendons. It is common to finish a time trial and not feel any pain but a day or so later come down with the nagging twinges of tendinitis. No matter how prepared you are for the event, an hour or so in a big gear can irritate your knees. Rolling around easily after the finish seems to help you avoid these delayed-action injuries better than immediate rest.

The more experienced you become as a rider, the more likely you are to spend the time to cool down on the bike. Phinney says he warms down as long as possible. "I think that a good long warm-down makes recovery from the effort easier and faster." Twigg says she "rolls around until my breathing isn't so fast and my legs aren't screaming." And Kiefel says he tries to ride about 10-15 miles.

You should have the usual massage, just as after any hard training effort. In addition Davis recommends a Jacuzzi, if possible. If the time trial is a long drive from your home and you are staying overnight in a motel, it is a good idea to treat yourself to one with a hot tub, Jacuzzi, or sauna for after the race. Indulgence will help your recovery, and thinking about that hedonistic pleasure in the last five miles of the race just might get you to the finish 30 seconds faster.

Evaluation of results

Finally, evaluate your performance. Don't, however, make the mistake of judging the success or failure of your ride and the training leading up to it solely on the basis of your time or your placing. These are important considerations but they have to be kept in perspective.

Instead I suggest that you replay the ride in your mind. Sitting in the Jacuzzi is not a bad time to do it. Evaluate your ride in three different categories by asking yourself some questions:

Category I: Effort and technique

1. Did I ride at top effort all the way? Was I willing to hurt to go faster? If not, what factors contributed? If so, how can I duplicate this advantageous situation for the next race?

2. If I concentrated well, what techniques did I use to stay focused on the event?

3. How was my performance of techniques: warmup, start, turnaround, etc.? What do I need to do in training to improve?

Category II: Results

1. How did my time compare to previous efforts? (This is the real test of your performance, but remember that your time can be strongly influenced by different courses as well as wind, temperature, humidity, altitude, and other factors.)

2. Where did I place? Am I improving in relation to other riders or am I losing ground?

Category III: Equipment

1. How did my equipment work?

2. How was my position on the bike?

3. If I used special TT equipment or modifications, were the changes positive or negative?

It is important to do this evaluation in an objective way. Emotions like frustration, guilt, or anger won't help you see how to improve and eliminate mistakes. Emotions only cloud your perceptions and goad you into self-defeating statements like: "I just can't force myself to ride harder and hurt more." Forcing yourself isn't the answer. You are doing this for fun, right? So find out, through objective analysis, why you didn't put out more effort and either accept it or figure out how to change the situation.

Getting angry at what you perceive as a poor performance is rarely a useful reaction and usually results in snap decisions like: "I'll train my guts out for two weeks and next time I'll blow all those guys away." And that decision leads, of course, to overtraining, exhaustion, and even slower times. So if you are self-coached, stand back and look at your performance as if you were someone else. If you have a coach, listen to the input in a similarly objective way. Then base your training for the next event on these rational decisions. As Eddie B says, "You have to be smart."

Many times a rider who lost by a small margin or missed breaking his PR by a second or two will look back on the time trial and see several places where he could have pushed a little harder or gained a tiny bit of time – enough to reach his goal. Such retrospections are fine. But don't fall into the trap of getting emotionally involved in the mistakes that you made during the time trial. Don't say, "What if I had done this or that?" There aren't any what-ifs, there is only what happened. Wishing and hoping won't change it. Direct your energies into making positive changes in your training to make sure such mistakes don't happen again.

The role of luck

As you can see, time trials are events that reward patience, dedication, and attention to detail. They are unlike road races, which can be influenced by the luck of crashes, chance position in the pack, and the selection process of widely varying terrain. Time trials seem to be a case of making your own luck through careful preparation.

But it doesn't always work that way. No matter how detailed your advance work, gremlins are going to pop out of odd corners to spoil your carefully laid plans. Even the best riders can be the victims of unforeseen problems. In the 1980 nationals a hard, early morning rain had soaked the parking area, the ground near the start, and the road. Eventual women's winner Beth Heiden got her cycling shoes wet and the sole became so flexible that she had trouble getting her cleats into the pedal properly at the start. With five seconds to go she was frantically asking if her cleats were in and she didn't get them engaged until she was a mile down the road. Despite losing some power at the start she rode 59:14.

The same year, defending record holder Sain punctured his rear tire just as he rode up to the line. A mechanic stuck in a new wheel but it was 20 seconds after his scheduled start when Sain finally got rolling. He didn't roll long. The rear wheel and cluster were incompatible with his bike and he tossed it into the roadside weeds in frustration.

21
Psychology

*Mental exercises to relax you
and bring out your best*

THE MORE faithfully you've done your training, the larger the psychological factors loom in time trialing. Two physically equal riders can be minutes apart at the end of 40 kilometers because of differences in their mental commitment to going fast on that day and in their ability to concentrate.

It's no secret that speed hurts, personal records can be painful, and winning against a top field requires you to continually push at the edge of extreme physical distress. You don't have to be a masochist or a martyr to do this well. You merely have to want to do it enough to accept it as a challenge. "Your motivation must be stronger than pain," Eddie B says. Phinney sees it not only as a personal challenge but also a kind of game. "I love to endlessly pursue extensions of my pain barrier."

But motivation is like strength, speed, and any other aspect of cycling performance. You won't be overflowing with it on the day of the race if you haven't practiced it in the weeks leading up to the event. The concentration that overcomes pain, fatigue, and self-doubt is a also a learned technique. Notice that I included self-doubt with pain and fatigue. If you go into a time trial doubting your ability, your preparation, or your mental readiness, you are beaten before you start.

The paradox of positive thinking

If there is one word that characterizes the mental approach of top time trialists it is "positive." Listen:

"Positive thinking." Kiefel.

"I have always used what is now called positive imaging." Haserot.

"I paint positive mental pictures about how the race is going to be." Shumway.

"I daydream about the race and how I want to ride. That must be positive imaging." Resh.

"I do some positive imagery of an entire race or time trial from start to finish." Ehlers.

But wait. Who are we kidding here? It is fine for top riders like Kiefel, Phinney, and Ehlers to talk about belief in the inevitability of their victory. They do win, frequently, and there is nothing like first place to convince you that you're good. But what about the rest of us who are less well-trained or talented? How do we go into a time trial believing we'll come out on top when past experience is loudly screaming the opposite?

Paradox time. All riders, even a Phinney or a Kiefel, are limited by their genetic potential. Some of us are quite limited. Coaches, teachers, generals, presidents, parents, and other moral leaders of society have long ignored that fact in their exhortations to their charges. "Nothing is impossible," they tell us. "You can be anything you want to be." These questionable assertions have rung through history and they have served a useful purpose in spite of their demonstrable lack of truth. Where would western civilization be if the Greeks at the Battle of Marathon hadn't believed that they could defeat the Persians who badly outnumbered them?

Once there was a 120-pound sophomore who wanted to be a fullback. The coach said "You can do whatever you set out to do. Run, lift weights, eat right, stick with me, and I'll make you a star." The kid threw his heart and soul into it. All winter, spring, and summer he pumped iron until his bench press went from 100 pounds to 180. He increased his squat to 210, his weight went up to 145, and his 40-yard dash time dropped to 5.1. It was an amazing physical transformation. But when the season began he was third string on the junior varsity. The varsity starter was a kid who didn't work out at all in the off-season, drank beer, and smoked funny-looking cigarettes, but was 6-foot-2, 195 pounds and hadn't run a 40 as slowly as 5.1 since he was in preschool. There ain't no justice.

The truth is that we aren't all equally endowed with athletic ability. I used the football story because physical size, 40-yard dash times, and bench-pressing ability are easily seen and measured. It's clear that one person is big and muscular while another isn't. Talents useful in cycling – like high oxygen uptake and an efficient oxygen transport system – are not as obvious. Cycling ability revolves around the number of mitochondria (thirsty little devils soaking up oxygen) in your cells. You can't tell what is going on at the cellular level by looking. But the principle is the same. There's those who have it, those who don't.

But, in an important sense, it really doesn't matter. Here's another one of those paradoxes: Although we know we are limited in our genetic potential, we can't allow ourselves to believe it. We have to train as if we were capable of world-class performances. If we believe that we are limited, we'll never come close to our potential. We have to convince ourselves, by an act of faith, that we have great potential and then train and race as if it were true.

Intellectually you may know that you'll never be a 52-minute time trialist. But at a much deeper level, the level of belief, you have to keep the faith. "You must believe in your ability to win," says Paulin. Otherwise, why bother?

Four-part mental exercises

The USCF thinks the mental component of training and racing is so important that it has a sports psychologist, Andy Jacobs, working with riders. I discussed the psychological side of cycling with him during a visit to the Olympic Training Camp. What he suggests for national team members is worth a try for anyone.

Jacobs says, "When you get on your bike, a lot of it is mental. The way your head works will determine how you will do. Your thoughts dictate your performance most of the time. A lot of athletes let themselves get worked up internally. They dwell on what they have to do and when you do that you start getting doubts and fears, negative thoughts that affect your concentration."

Jacobs uses a mental exercise with OTC riders to help them relax, focus their thoughts on training or racing, and be positive. I'll describe below how to do each part. These techniques are somewhat difficult to learn from a book but can be picked up rapidly if you have a qualified person to guide you through the steps. So it might be a good idea to find a sports psychologist in your area. They can be hard to find. Jacobs says that "there are fewer than 50 competent people doing what I'm doing in this country right now." This situation is changing as more athletes see the need for psychological as well as physical coaching, but at present most athletes will have to learn from printed instructions.

Another method of accomplishing the same thing is through transcendental meditation or some form of Eastern religious techniques. Pro rider Tom Prehn is an advocate of TM and he rode a 53:14 in the 1982 Colorado district TT so something was working for him.

Some riders do their mental workouts before breakfast. They check their morning heart rate while still in bed, then get up and do some stretching exercises. Those are followed by the mental exercises. You can also do them at night just after you go to bed. They are great to help you relax and fall asleep, especially if you are still wired up from a race or hard training ride.

According to Jacobs, "The general exercise for cyclists has four parts. First is a breathing exercise to help you relax." Sit or lie in a comfortable position. Be sure you are warm enough. If it is chilly, drape a blanket over your shoulders. Close your eyes and take normal breaths, concentrating on breathing from your diaphraghm instead of your chest. Let your thoughts flow freely with no conscious effort to control them. Continue for several minutes until you feel relaxed and rhythmical.

Jacobs continues. "Then we go to a progressive muscle relaxation exercise starting at the feet and tightening different muscles, then loosening them. This relaxes the rider." Start by tightening the muscles in your calves, then relax slowly while counting backwards from ten. When you reach one, all the tension should be washed out of your lower legs. Do the same thing for the following muscle groups in order: the quadriceps and hamstrings, the gluteals, the lower back, abdominals, arms, chest, upper shoulders (trapezius), neck, and facial muscles.

Tighten each set of muscles in turn and relax them slowly and progressively. While you are doing this, continue your steady diaphragm breathing. Pay particular attention to the muscle groups in the lower back, upper shoulders, neck, and face because these areas are typically where tension surfaces first. According to Jacobs, this procedure "relaxes the muscles even further and teaches riders about muscle tension so they can recognize it and get rid of it in a race.

"Then," says Jacobs, "we do a guided fantasy. I'll take them mentally to a place that is very peaceful, quiet, confident – the mountains or the beach. It is a place they can come to in their heads before a race. They can instill the confidence that comes from thinking about that place."

Of course, it is helpful to have your own psychologist to talk you to your personal mental hideaway, but it isn't necessary. Just imagine a place that is relaxing and peaceful to you and mentally go there. Allow yourself to get totally immersed in the place. If it is in the mountains, smell the air, the flowers, the pine needles, and

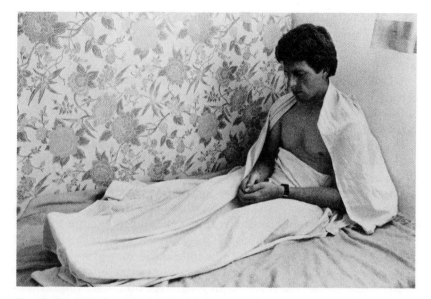

Tom Prehn, '86 U.S. professional road champion, is one of a growing number of athletes using mental techniques for relaxation, motivation, and a competitive edge.

watch the big puffy clouds float over the peaks. Be there.

"Finally I take them through an actual visualization of the race, the way they want to ride it, going through the specific things they want to do." Again, you can visualize the race yourself. Imagine the whole sequence of a time trial from warmup to finish. Visualize yourself doing everything well. You start powerfully, keep your cadence up, and handle the turnaround like a pro. Sports psychologists say that you shouldn't see yourself from the outside like you were on a videotape, but rather from inside. Look at the steps in the time trial from your own eyes as if you were actually riding it.

All these mental techiques take practice and there are several pitfalls. One is that some riders begin to visualize the race and get tense. The very thought of racing makes them nervous and all the relaxation they have accumulated in steps one, two, and three goes out the window. I asked Jacobs how to combat this and also the attendant danger, that you'll perversely start to visualize everything in the race going wrong. He replied, "If that happens I tell them to go back and relax again. Actually I've told some riders to picture the race with everything going wrong. Then I have them turn around and see what they need to do if they have a bad start or lose

their concentration or find that pain is getting to them. We focus
on why that is happening and what they can do about it."

Before and during the race

These techniques also work just before you start your warmup for
a race. However, some riders are afraid that they will be too relaxed
to perform well if they try it.

I asked Andy if a time trialer should be relaxed or aggressive before a race. The answer, not surprisingly, was a paradox. "You can
feel relaxed and aggressive at the same time. There is a peak level
of arousal. If you take a bell curve, the left side of the curve as you
go up is where you need to use motivation and goals to get you
psyched up. The peak of the curve is where you are at your optimum
level – aggressive and concentrating, yet relaxed enough to focus.
If you go past that peak you are going to get too psyched up and
tense. That is where negative thoughts come in."

During the actual race, the rule is to concentrate on going fast.
If the event is short to medium in length (10-50 miles) you need to
practice focusing all your thoughts on keeping your level of exertion
right on the edge of your anaerobic threshold. In longer time trials,
the same continual concentration is necessary to be sure that you
apportion your energy so it lasts the distance. In both cases, that
means you have to concentrate on the pain you are experiencing instead of thinking about something else that is more pleasant.

William Morgan, a sports psychologist, studied endurance athletes and found that the elite performers used a technique he calls
association. They concentrate on their burning lungs or throbbing
legs, they continually try to push their speed higher, and they are
always monitoring how they feel.

Less successful performers used disassociation, according to Morgan. They tried to escape the pain and effort during a race by thinking about pleasant surroundings, chanting mantras, or doing complex mathematical puzzles in their head.

The elite athlete, in other words, is more in tune with his surroundings and his feelings. He is willing to face the pain and effort
honestly and try to beat it. Most important of all he is willing to
look his limits in the eye and try to push them back.

Recently Morgan has done more studies and now states that although association is the preferred strategy for elite athletes, a
little disassociation at crucial times in a race can be helpful even
for top performers. But he still maintains that the primary cogni-

tive strategy for the best endurance athletes is association. That is certainly borne out by the comments of successful cyclists like Phinney: "I continually monitor my body during a time trial." Davis is obviously not running from the pain. Instead he welcomes it as a gauge of his speed and energy output.

22

Injuries

Treat minor problems yourself,
see a doctor for more serious ones

BIKE RACING is a relatively safe sport and any medical problems
are usually minor. However, they can escalate rapidly if they aren't
treated properly. That's because, in an athlete, much of the energy
that usually heals minor injuries and infections is being used for
training and adaptation to greater and greater performance demands. As a result, it pays to know about the common medical problems that affect cyclists and what to do about them.

Saddle sores

Saddle sores are skin eruptions — boils or pimples — that are
caused by the germs always present on your skin. If your tender
epidermis gets irritated by contact with the saddle, these bacteria
can enter. The resulting infection makes it uncomfortable or impossible to ride. You have to be tough to be a bike racer but who wants
to ride 75 miles on an open boil?

Even the European pros are plagued by this malady and some
desperate remedies have been tried to keep a rider in action. American novelist Ernest Hemingway, an enthusiastic observer of the cycling scene when he lived in Paris during the 1920s, wrote about
a rider in his novel *The Sun Also Rises*. At dinner before an important stage "he sat on the small of his back [and] the other riders
joked him about his boils. . . . 'Listen,' he said, 'tomorrow my nose
is so tight on the handlebars that the only thing touches those boils
is a lovely breeze.' "

Other riders who didn't feel like doing a 120-mile race out of the
saddle have sat on a thin piece of raw steak or made a donut out
of orthopedic felt or foam. Some have resorted to novocaine injections to get them through important races. Merckx had to undergo
operations to remove the cysts that had formed because he ignored
the pain and continued to ride on severe boils.

Obviously the way to avoid such misery is to keep saddle sores from forming in the first place. The secret to that is cleanliness. Before every ride, wash your crotch area thoroughly with mild soap on a washcloth. This cuts down on the population of the wee beasties that live on your skin waiting for a gap in your defenses.

Have enough shorts so you can wash them frequently and wear a clean pair for every ride. Nothing can cause a skin eruption the size of Mount St. Helens faster than wearing shorts with a dirty chamois stiffened with sweat. Also, a chamois that has been washed frequently loses its natural oils and soon has the texture of a taco chip. You can avoid too-frequent washings by cleaning the chamois after each ride with alcohol and a washcloth.

Some riders swear by a lubricating and antiseptic salve to rub on a leather chamois. This is available commercially or you can make your own with a mixture of ingredients available at the local drug store: A&D ointment, vaseline, lanolin, and cod-liver oil. Experiment with the proportion of these components until you get a consistency slightly thicker and more viscous than vaseline alone. The resulting goo works great but if you use too much cod-liver oil, it smells like you are concealing a dead fish in your shorts.

Some cycling shorts come with an artificial chamois made of material that looks like a fine pile or terry cloth. It used to be an inexpensive substitute for the real thing. But it has been improved recently and now seems to work almost as well as leather. Some riders have an allergy to real chamois. For them, changing to the synthetic variety has cleared up some intractable cases of saddle sores almost immediately. And the synthetic version offers the advantage of easy care. Just wash the shorts and the artificial chamois dries right along with the rest of the fabric.

An alternative is no chamois at all. Top Canadian rider Genny Brunet says, "Chamois is a throwback to when shorts were wool and you needed something in there because of the abrasive material. Now, with the smooth Lycra fabric, the chamois isn't needed. Besides, it irritates me."

After a ride or race don't stand around in damp clammy shorts while the resident bugs storm the defenses of your irritated breech. Instead, repeat the wash and change into street clothes. There are rarely dressing rooms available at races so try a restroom or the front seat of the car. Modesty has to give way to necessity in this case. I always carry alcohol and a washcloth in my racing kit and have found that this treatment cuts the possibility of problems to almost zero.

If you do get saddle sores despite all these measures, suspect over-training. Long-term fatigue can cause your body's defenses to break down at their weakest point. If your tender skin has been chafed on a saddle for several hours, that is probably your weakest point. Persistent saddle sores, if you have followed the rules of cleanliness faithfully, can often indicate that you've overdone your training. Painful as they can be, they are merely harbingers of bigger trouble ahead (or behind).

If you develop a boil it is best to take several days off, both to rest your body and let its natural defenses regenerate and to get pressure off the infected area. Continued riding can drive the infection deep into the tissues. So can trying to break boils that have come to a head – this is best left to a doctor. A severe case can consist of one or two primary boils and half a dozen others that sprout at random, the result of secondary infection.

Some riders use a general antibiotic salve to treat open boils. I've had success with Campo-Phenique in salve form spread on the irritated areas, before they boil over so to speak, as well as for use on the real thing. In any case, do your best to avoid boils so severe that they need to be lanced. However, if you ever have to have it done, this advice will be forever after unnecessary.

Tendinitis

Another common cyclist's injury is tendinitis. This can be caused by overuse early in the season if you increase your mileage too rapidly. Another cause is a badly adjusted cleat position or a saddle that is too low or too high. Pushing a big gear before you are ready will do it also. Time trialists, with their penchant for the big ring, need to be especially wary.

Direct irritation can cause tendinitis too. According to Paige Leddington, assistant trainer at the Olympic Training Camp, national team pursuiter Dave Grylls had a mysterious case of Achilles tendinitis that baffled a whole team of sports medicine sleuths. It was cleared up only when they realized that the zipper on his winter overboots was subtly poking at the tendon.

Treatment? According to Leddington, "We probably use ultrasound more on cyclists than anyone else (for) Achilles tendinitis and patellar tendinitis." If you don't have the Olympic sports medicine facility handy, you can probably get treatments at a local sports medicine clinic or a chiropractor.

I have found ice and aspirin to be useful in heading off trouble, used at the first sign of a twinge after a ride. Don't be afraid to take a day off either. A day lost now could save you a month later. My longest layoff from training in 11 years, except for the usual rest days, was a more than two-month siege caused by inflammation of a small tendon near the patella. It was initially irritated when I ran an off-season marathon for training. It got worse when I tried to get back on the bike too soon. I eventually had to resort to cortisone injections to clear up the problem. Because such treatment can have severe side effects it is a situation I've taken pains to never let develop again.

Cold can initiate or aggravate tendinitis problems in some riders. When you're training it is prudent to keep your knees covered in temperatures below about 65 degrees, or even when it is warmer if you suspect trouble.

Road rash

Time trialists are less apt than road racers to develop a sudden case of the lacerations and abrasions that is euphemistically called road rash. But any rider who is training hard is going to misjudge his limits occasionally and go down, collecting a sample. Most falls are sliding affairs so the painful abrasions are relatively minor and limited to one side of the body. That is a great advantage because you can sleep or rest on the uninjured side. If you tumble, you are likely to lose skin in patches all over and when you try to sleep you'll stick unpleasantly to the sheets.

Because road surfaces are so dirty, be sure to have a tetanus shot or booster periodically. Treat abrasions by icing them down to reduce swelling and scrubbing them thoroughly as soon as possible. The foaming action of hydrogen peroxide works well but regular soap will do the trick too. In either case you'll have to grit your teeth and scrub to get the road dirt out. Use a washcloth or a pliable plastic brush. If you don't, you run an increased risk of infection. And those dark-colored, embedded pieces of grit will heal up in the wound making your leg look like you've been to a drunk tatooist.

If you repeat the cleansing process several times a day on wounds located where you can expose them to the air, most minor cases of road rash will heal properly with only this treatment. Coating the abrasions with antibiotic salve helps prevent infection, makes the wound's surface pliable, and less likely to crack open painfully. You can also cover the wound with a non-stick pad if you have to put clothes over it. It is best to leave it uncovered, however, so the air can get to it.

Abrasions are usually accompanied by scrapes on the outside of your legs and knees. Nearly all racers, male and female, shave their legs to make these wounds easier to scrub out. The theory goes that hair will catch on the road and increase the size of the injury while smooth skin will slide. I am not sure about that, but I find that scrapes tend to heal better with less chance of infection if I am shaved down. Smooth skin makes massage easier too. Time trial specialists or triathletes are less likely to shave, seeing it as an affectation or a display of vanity since muscle definition and vascularity show up better on hairless legs.

I think it is a personal decision. Don't do it if you feel uncomfortable, imagining that you will be the target of sidelong stares or snide remarks. If you decide to take the plunge, harvest your hairy legs down to the stubble the first time with a set of electric clippers, then shave. If you try a blade initially you'll be at the task forever as the razor clogs up on the long hair every stroke or two.

You can also minimize the effects of a crash on your upper body by wearing a shirt under your jersey. One layer will slide against the other and dissipate some of the friction away from your skin. A lightweight, sleeveless wool vest works well, particularly with Lycra jerseys, since they slide easily on the wool. Polypropylene works well too.

It is the opinion of some experienced crashees that Lycra shorts, even with nothing underneath, seem to reduce damage to the underlying skin compared to wool shorts. This may be due to the smoother, less irritating feel of the material or to the way it clings like a second skin. My experience seems to bear that out. I once crashed in Lycra shorts and, although the heat from the friction of my slide literally melted a hole in the shorts, the damage to my skin was quite a bit less than I expected. Even though the pavement was rough, the wound was smooth, more like a burn than the usual abrasion that is scored with deeper lacerations from uneven macadam. In fact, abrasions resemble burns closely so the new "second skin" marketed for use on blisters and burns is also useful for treating road rash.

Another result of a crash is usually some sort of contusion or bruise. Ice is the treatment here. You'll probably be sore all over after a spill because of the violent shock of landing and because your muscles will contract spontaneously and powerfully in an attempt to absorb the blow. Getting back on the bike and riding easily as soon as possible after a crash will loosen up the afflicted muscles and speed recovery.

Other problems

For more serious problems like extensive road rash, head injuries, or suspected broken bones, see a doctor, preferably one experienced in the treatment of athletic injuries. He will be more likely to tell you to rehabilitate by riding your bike instead of instructing you to rest for three weeks to cure the patch of road rash on your knee.

Head injuries are a danger in cycling but they can be largely prevented if you wear a good hardshell helmet every time you ride. They are required in USCF-sanctioned events. Don't think that you don't need one because you are a time trialist and therefore less prone to crashes. Crashes in time trials are often head-first affairs caused by hitting an obstruction that you don't see while going all out.

Time trialists are also subject to the dreaded numb crotch caused by the pressure of the saddle in one place for long periods of time. Road riders tend to be out of the saddle frequently on climbs and jumps. But a time trialist sits down and grinds away for an hour or more and the whole crotch area can lose all feeling temporarily. This can make cycling a real dead end. One cure is to change position frequently in training. Be sure your saddle is comfortable. You may have to try different brands until you find one that doesn't produce symptoms in you.

Saddle position is important too. If it is too far back you'll always be sliding forward onto the narrow tip which will press on the nerves more than the broad rear of the saddle would. You may have to lower the tip of the saddle slightly too since you'll be on the drops more than a road rider who varies his hand position for climbs, jams, and rolling along in the pack.

Whatever is causing your symptoms, find and eliminate it. Persisting to ride under these conditions can lead to the sort of serious problems that you wouldn't wish on your worst enemy.

Some riders suffer from numb hands because the weight of their upper body on the handlebars compresses a nerve. If your position on the bike is good, this shouldn't be a problem. If it is, padded handlebar tape and well-padded cycling gloves usually work.

Good position on the bike also alleviates another common complaint of many riders – a sore lower back or sore shoulders. These aches arise at the beginning of the season if you have been off the bike awhile due to bad weather. A few weeks of riding usually eliminates the problem. Strengthening your back, neck, and shoulders with a good weight training program will probably eliminate these complaints permanently.

Massage

One useful therapeutic technique that will help you recover faster from training or racing is massage. Long used in Europe, massage seemed to me one of those arcane continental gimmicks, more psychological than physical. Like most riders who don't have a team masseur, I always meant to use massage but somehow never got around to it regularly. This season I have been using self-massage after every hard ride and have discovered what the European riders have always known – it really does work.

Although it would be great to have a real soigneur work over your quads or be schooled in all the subtle differences in technique, neither of these luxuries is necessary. You can do a perfectly adequate job yourself.

Shaved legs are much easier to massage than hairy ones and are less apt to develop small infections from irritating the hair follicles. Use a massage cream or a drug store substitute like Albolene, normally used for skin cleansing. In the winter I like a combination of alcohol, witch hazel, baby oil, and oil of wintergreen to provide a warming effect.

Sit on a towel and start with your feet, rubbing the toes and soles with circular motions, then the calves, kneading them upwards toward the heart. Finish off with the quads and spend most of your time on them because they do most of the work in cycling. Seated on the floor, legs in front, you can get the weight of your upper body into it and really work those muscles over. Don't massage so vigorously that you injure tissue, but knead and rub the quads, again pulling upwards toward the heart. Ten minutes spent each evening will work wonders in making your recovery from hard training faster.

Compared to the pounding of running or to contact sports like football, cycling is a remarkably injury-free activity. One study found that cyclists were more fit than other athletes because they

Massage can help you recover faster from training and racing. If you're not so fortunate as to have a skilled masseur available, you can use the self-massage system described here.

were able to exercise more consistently without periodic interruption due to injury. The secret to improvement is steady increases in work load over a long period of time, a goal you'll be better able to achieve if you treat the occasional cycling malady quickly and effectively.

23
Nutrition

*Eat wisely, because food is the fuel
for your training and racing*

NUTRITION FOR the time trialist is the same as for any other athlete. Eat a wide variety of food in sufficient quantities to give you the energy you need to fuel your training miles. Avoid fad foods, purported nutritional miracles, and highly processed foods.

Variety is important to get the nutrients you need. If you limit your diet to half a dozen food choices you may miss out on some essential vitamins or minerals. There's nothing wrong with a meal restricted to brown rice, one vegetable, and an apple for dessert. But you are taking a big nutritional gamble if you try to live on that three times a day for a month. It's the same with a hamburger and fries. They're okay occasionally (very occasionally) but five times a week and your arteries may start to look like clogged-up grease traps. Eat a wide variety of foods with moderation.

The same approach works for the amount you eat. Don't restrict your food intake in the belief that you'll be a better rider if you are extremely thin. Once you are training regularly and your weight stabilizes, trying to get even lighter by dieting is likely to result in a loss of muscle tissue rather than fat. If you have been training regularly 200 miles a week or so and eating wisely, you probably have reached a weight and body-fat percent that is right for you. When that happens, let it be.

I know a stocky, muscular rider who came into cycling from a background in football weighing 205. Within a year of beginning to train for racing his weight had dropped to 170 pounds due to the miles alone. He was strong as a horse and successful at all sorts of races. His percent of body fat was 9.5. But he wasn't satisfied with his climbing so he went on a diet and dropped another 20 pounds. At 150, his body fat had only decreased to 8.5% so most of his weight loss was the muscle that had propelled him up the road. At 170 he had looked like a muscular former football player with big, defined thighs and shoulders. At 150 he looked like a very ill anorexic. He lost his power on the bike, his energy for the affairs of life, and the last flicker of a desire to race. Recovery was slow and tedious.

As a time trialist, your stock in trade is the power to push big gears for a long time and the vigor and energy to sustain a high work output. Eddie B calls time trialing "an event of work, not speed." And that is precisely what it is — plenty of old-fashioned hard work. Why do so many riders think they can adhere to a restrictive diet and still have the energy to train well, the muscle mass to go fast?

There is a bit of a paradox here. You have to eat large quantities of food to get the nutrients that you need. But if you eat like a lumberjack, you'll get fat — unless you also exercise like one. Then you get lean and strong. Hard exercise is the catalyst that changes calories into energy, muscles, and performance.

This is no license to overeat or to eat indiscriminately. Eat a wide variety of foods in moderate quantities, train hard, and let your body fat and weight take care of itself, even if you are an all-rounder who wants to climb well in road races. If you think that you are too stocky, you'll just have to live with your physique. Once you have reached your body's natural limits of body fat and muscle bulk — even if you still look like the Hulk — you won't be able to go lower without dieting and compromising performance. Accept the physical parameters you can't change and improve your performance by training, not by dietary manipulation.

Because food is an ally, not the enemy, establish a bilateral pact with bread, potatoes, pasta, vegetables, and fruit; an embassy next to the produce section of your food store; diplomatic relations with carbohydrates. Deploy a multi-nutritional force to help you perform at your best. An unnecessarily restrictive diet is a rider's window of vulnerability.

There is another advantage to being flexible in your eating habits. Bike racing usually involves travel, and when you are on the road it is difficult to find specialized food. What does a vegetarian do at a truck stop off I-70 in Kansas? Casebeer says, "I don't like being dependent on one diet. If you eat a certain type of food all the time, then can't get it, your body could react poorly and affect your performance. Eat a variety of foods — it helps keep your body more stable."

Vitamin supplements

There is one qualification to the idea that a normal, balanced diet will fulfill all your nutritional needs. The Soviets feel that elite athletes need vitamins, minerals, and trace-element supplementation in their diets. According to Michael Yessis, editor of *Soviet Sports Review*, "The Soviets say there is no way in the world a normal, good diet is going to replace what these guys use in workouts. They've found that the high-level athlete is a different breed. They have to treat him differently."

And many riders, even if they aren't elite performers, argue that any cyclist needs supplementation if he is performing at his peak levels. The theory goes that if a world-class athlete capable of exerting himself 100% in training and racing can do a 52-minute 40km ride, then a part-time athlete who puts out 100% to ride a 1:02 needs extra vitamins and minerals too. The degree to which you approach your limits is the key, according to this view, not the final result on the clock, since that varies widely according to innate ability.

In fact, a recreational racer who trains hard 200 or so miles a week, has a job, and fits in a family life might need supplements more than the elite Soviet cyclist who rides four or five hours a day and spends the rest of the time recuperating under the watchful eyes of a team of sports medicine professionals. So you'll have to decide whether a vitamin supplement might be helpful. Multivitamins probably can't hurt, but megadoses of some vitamins are known to be harmful. Again, moderation is the watchword.

Eating before the race

Eating before a time trial is a matter of personal preference and is dictated by the length of the race. If it is a 100-miler or a 24-hour event, eat plenty and don't stop when the race begins. You'll need it. On his transcontinental rides former record holder Lon Haldeman is notorious for eating anything that doesn't bite him first, including a wide assortment of processed foods. The pace is slow enough on these ultradistance events that most riders can get down about anything.

Shorter time trials require such a violent, sustained effort from the start that your stomach should be virtually empty or you're liable to have your breakfast decorating your handlebars. The general rule is to eat a light high-carbohydrate meal about four hours before the start of a 10- to 50-mile time trial. Exercise physiologist David

Costill recommends cereal with sugar and milk, juice, and toast for marathoners and that is probably the right combination for cyclists too.

But don't deny your preferences just because the latest study recommends something that you detest. You have to feel good about what you are eating before a race and if cereal makes you gag, that's a poor way to start the day. Your body may rebel too. I usually prefer a banana on my cereal rather than sugar but some people can't digest bananas well and four hours later it is still down there, going along for the ride.

Many people like coffee in the morning and can't face a normal day without it, much less the stress of a race. According to research done by Dr. Costill the caffeine is supposed to release free fatty acids and increase endurance. This effect seems to be limited in riders who drink coffee as part of their normal routine. If you aren't used to it you may develop an upset stomach, diarrhea, or increased urinary flow instead of greater endurance. You won't go very fast if you are looking for roadside bushes.

Some riders find that caffeine helps them get mentally ready. "I find coffee and Coke to be beneficial in terms of getting me pumped up for a hard effort," says Phinney. However, top time trialists generally agree that the caffeine in coffee isn't an aid to performance. "I have to have some coffee to wake up," confesses Ehlers, "but I don't think it aids me physically in a race."

Paulin likes "coffee for getting up early and going to the bathroom [but] performance? No way."

Caffeine is also available in more concentrated pill form but few riders experience any benefit. "I tried a half a caffeine pill before Vail [the time trial in the Coors Classic] one year and I wouldn't do it again," reveals Twigg. "I was too nervous and I could have gotten stomach cramps or something."

Haserot agrees, saying, "I have played around with No-Doz [but] have done my best racing unaided by such things."

So it is safest to eat and drink what you normally do before a time trial. The body likes regularity, it hates surprises, and it will lash back if you surprise it too often.

During the race
Food or liquid during the race? For 5- to 25-mile time trials, you usually don't need to eat or drink. Potoff says "I don't even have the braze-ons for a bottle bracket cage on my TT frame. [For short

Amateur and professional hour record holders Hans Henrik Oersted and Francesco Moser know the importance of fluid replacement during longer events. Though their equipment is the lightest and sleekest, they still carry water bottles during the classic two-man time trial, the 96km Baracchi Trophy in Italy. Moser, right, helped legitimize aerodynamic equipment when he broke the 12-year-old pro hour record in 1984.

events] it would be excessive weight and wind drag and a distraction. And there is no time to take a drink."

Somewhere around 30 miles you need to drink something during the race and in events like the 100km team time trial or the cycling leg of long triathlons it is important to take something along even if you don't anticipate using it. Potoff says that if it is warm on a long time trial he will take two bottles.

Eddie B suggests, "When you are wearing a skinsuit make a pocket out of your number and carry a little food." Sliced and peeled apples are good and many riders like orange sections. Whatever you use, be sure you've tested it thoroughly in training. Even then there is no guarantee. Only experience will show you what you can tolerate in race conditions.

I find that diluted commercial electrolyte replacement drinks, diluted defizzed Coke, or diluted apple juice go well on long hot training rides even when I'm pushing hard. But in a race the same mixture tastes bad enough to gag a maggot. I haven't figured out whether this is due to the increased exertion level of racing or is a psychological phenomenon caused by the stress of competition. I do know that in most cases I'd better drink plain water or risk disaster.

Eating and traveling

Unless you live in a major racing area it is likely that at least a few times a year you will have to travel some distance to a race – perhaps even the day before the event. Be sure to eat and drink enough on the trip. Some riders are afraid of gaining weight so they cut their food intake drastically on their rest or travel days. You need the energy that food gives even more the day before a race. If you have been eating moderately from a wide variety of foods and have been putting in your miles, you won't get fat in one day. But if you don't eat, your blood sugar will plummet, you may get carsick on curvy roads (to the dismay of your traveling companions) and you might be listless for the race.

The eating rule while traveling is to eat little and often. Snack frequently during the trip on dried or fresh fruit, nuts, or wholegrain bread instead of stopping once for a big greasy meal at some roadside ptomaine palace. Eat what you are used to on the trip. The day before the race is a poor time to change your dietary habits.

Drink plenty of water too. Cars can be pretty hot places. Even if you don't think you are perspiring that much, you are probably losing fluids at a substantial rate. Surprisingly, the effect is increased by air conditioning because it dries the perspiration before you notice it and because the air blown out by air-conditioning systems is often less humid than the outside air. This resulting drying effect can dehydrate you in a hurry and you don't want to start the race feeling like a raisin.

More travel tips

While I am on the subject of travel, here are a few more health tips. If you have to travel quite a distance by car to the race, try to go the night before. Don't get up at 2 a.m., drive four or five hours, and expect to do well when you race at eight or nine in the morning. Your body probably isn't used to sitting in a cramped position for long. The result of those hours in the car can be legs so swollen and stiff that you'll need more than a pre-race warmup to get them back to normal.

Travel by car is much more demanding than it appears and one rule of racers who gypsy around the country from race to race is: Never count a travel day as a rest day. You may not be riding the bike, but if you're a fit rider used to activity, six hours in someone's subcompact and you'll wish you had been. As one rider put it: "You get tired doing nothing."

Be sure to allow yourself plenty of time. You don't want to add to the stress of the trip by being late and having to drive too fast. There will be enough danger and excitement in the event itself without turning the highway into a time trial course. Running late frays your nerves, too, wasting energy better kept for the ride. You want to race the clock in competition, not on the way to the start.

Sufficient time also allows you more leisure to stop along the way every hour or so and move around. Stretch, walk around the car, or do a few push-ups – anything to get your system moving again.

Try to avoid stressful conversations during the drive. Traveling to a race is no place to iron out animosity among teammates or family members. Relax, listen to music, look at the scenery.

If you have a choice, drive the afternoon or evening before the race and stay in a motel near the course. Get there early enough to roll around in an easy gear for half an hour before dinner, checking out the turnaround area on the course and noting any hazards or potential trouble spots. A little exercise will work wonders in clearing the travel haze from your head and the kinks from your legs.

Before you go to bed lay everything out you'll need for the next morning. Most time trials start early and it is easy to go off in a rush at 6 a.m. leaving something crucial behind. A personal checklist is a good idea. Include such standard items as your bike, race wheels, pump, cycling shoes, and helmet but also less obvious ones like your USCF license, pins for your number, and money for registration.

Also include on your list any personal items that could be labeled idiosyncrasies but without which you'd feel lost. I know one rider who claims that he can't race well without a couple of swigs of his favorite electrolyte replacement drink several minutes before the start. Another tapes down his shoe laces. If he forgets the tape, he is forlorn indeed. Whatever your personal security blanket, include it in your list.

24
Equipment

Got money to spend for more speed?
Light wheels should be first choice

THE 1984 U.S. OLYMPIC team time trial bikes had 24-inch front wheels with 14 spokes and 27-inch rear wheels with 28 spokes. They sported 120-gram tires inflated with helium to more than 130 pounds. Moser broke Merckx's hour record on a similar bike with turned-up handlebars and shielded spokes. The best time trialer in your town races on a tricked-out model so light he has to tether it down before the start. How can you compete against all this technology on your old reliable road bike?

You can't — at least, not strictly speaking. Expensive aerodynamic frames and components are an advantage because fighting wind resistance saps most of your energy production at 25 m.p.h. Although the streamlining effect of aero frames and helmets may not be as great as some manufacturers want you to believe, it does exist.

But there is another side to the picture. Although an aerodynamic bike alone has significantly less wind resistance in wind-tunnel tests compared to a regular bike, most of the advantage evaporates when a rider is included. Your body presents a much greater frontal area than a bike frame and your pumping legs introduce turbulence that negates much of the aerodynamic effect of certain components.

Potoff maintains, "I've read honest evaluations that state that a cyclist, even on the drops, has more wind resistance than an F-104 jet interceptor. A rider's body has more surface area than any improvement aero components can [negate]. I see little connection between the outlandish claims component and frame makers have made and actual performances." And Phinney adds, "I think for individual time trialing aero bikes are useless. The rider displaces so much more air that the bike is secondary."

So those fancy Olympic bikes are an advantage but the time gain

is measured in fractions of a second. Although this may be significant in top international competition, when was the last time you
lost a time trial by even one second, much less a tenth or a hundredth? On the other hand, your training makes significant
changes in your time. On most levels of racing it is the rider, not
the bike, that is the key component. As Kiefel says, "You need aero
stuff to compete on the international level. But what is important
is what is in the legs and heart." Hammer agrees that "aerodynamic
equipment helps but fitness and body position are more important."
And Resh has a practical suggestion: "It would be better not to
spend the money on aero equipment, work fewer hours, and train
more."

There are plenty of ways to make your present bike and clothing
as fast and aerodynamic as possible. Your riding position is important. I discussed this in an earlier chapter but a reminder here:
Tucking your elbows in out of the wind lessens your drag far more
than fancy aero rims ($150), an aero frameset ($600-1,000), or a
"cone-head" helmet ($50-100). A little time spent on position can
save you seconds as well as dollars. Sipay is no stranger to high-tech
equipment, but he agrees that proper position is the most effective
thing you can do to reduce wind resistance.

Light wheels

If your riding position is as streamlined as it can be and you want
to invest in equipment, Sipay recommends a light set of wheels. Because wheels and tires represent rolling resistance, they are the
most vital components on the bike, the soul of your time trialing
machine. Phinney says, "Wheels are important to me. Stiff, 28
spokes (oval) with light rims and 195-gram tires are what the
7-Eleven [team] uses. It is a great psychological boost to get on those
after warming up on training wheels."

As with any other component, the more you decrease the weight
the more you lose strength and increase the risk of mechanical trouble. "First you have to get to the finish line," Sipay says. "And if
12 spokes are going to save you a hundredth of a second and you
don't make it because you are trying to save that hundredth of a
second, then what good is it?"

On the conservative side you can use a regular road racing ensemble: 32- or 36-hole rims and 250-gram tires, especially on rough
roads. The next lighter setup, like the one Phinney mentions, fea-
tures 28-hole hubs, narrow rims like the Mavic CX 18, and light

Streamlining your riding position is a greater aerodynamic improvement than the fanciest equipment. But if you have money to invest, light wheels are a good choice and so is a skinsuit. World champion Rebecca Twigg uses a long-sleeved version in the 3,000-meter pursuit.

narrow-profile tires like the Wolber Record Route 18. Don't go too light. Kiefel says, "Light wheels are the most important component. The lighter the better, but it better be strong." Potoff says he learned the importance of strength the hard way. He tried extremely light wheels and broke spokes in both the front and rear wheels. "The weight I saved was totally lost when the components failed."

Some riders go with as few as 24 spokes. Sipay recommends radial spoking in front "and as few spokes as you can get away with in the rear, with radial and cross one or two on the drive side."

Are such wheels really an advantage? I had an opportunity to find out on a visit to the Olympic Training Camp in Colorado Springs. When I arrived I discovered there was a 10-mile time trial taking place that weekend. Sipay was there and he offered to put light wheels on my bike so I could see what a difference they made.

The wheels, used by the U.S. team in the world championships, sported 24 spokes, radial on the front. The rear was cross two on the drive side and cross one on the other. The rims were V-shaped Assos aerodynamic complete with Wolber Record Route 18 170-gram tires. The wheels looked fragile with all that space between the spokes and those skinny tires. I wondered how I would get back to the start if I hit some imperceptible bump in the road and the wheels disintegrated, spokes flying one direction, the pretzelled rim rolling crazily in the other.

The wheels felt fast when I warmed up but during the race that feeling evaporated. When you are pushing hard, it hurts the same whether you are going 28 m.p.h. on light wheels or 26 m.p.h. on heavy ones. Sipay had assured me of their durability and he was right. Not even my snorting, stomping charge away from the line or a jam up the last little hill produced so much as a wobble in either wheel.

I have always time trialed on regular road wheels and tires, believing that their durability and stiffness are more important than taking a chance on ultra-light equipment. I've always believed that fitness and mental attitude are far more important than trick equipment.

However, a serious time trialist who wants to pull out all the stops for an important event might want to invest in a set of wheels like the ones I tried, which may cost upwards of $350. It can be a problem finding someone qualified to build such light wheels with uncommon spoking patterns. As Sipay notes, you need to have confidence in your wheelbuilder if your district or national championship hopes are riding on his product.

For most riders the question of whether to get a pair of these wheels is academic. They are too expensive for the two or three times a season they would be used. For time trials I'll stick to a traditional lightweight set of road wheels: 32 holes, 290-gram rims, 15-gauge spokes laced three cross, and 220-gram tires that will hold 130-140 pounds of pressure. For longer time trials, rough roads, or triathlons, an even heavier ensemble might be worth its weight in added durability.

Clincher tire technology is improving all the time and there are some reasons to consider a set of these wheels for time trials. Studies have shown that some bald narrow clinchers with supple casings have less rolling resistance than the best tubulars. Pan Am gold medalist Rory O'Reilly used them in setting world records on the track, and top professional Sean Kelly has been experimenting with clinchers in European racing.

Clincher tires are generally less expensive and are easier to repair than tubulars because the tubes can be replaced. Latex tubes are lightest, and if you use talc when installing them you can avoid pinching the tube beneath the tire bead. One disadvantage of clincher wheels is the currently available rims, which are generally heavy and hard to find in anything less than a 32-hole configuration.

Disk wheels are another option that's received a lot of attention lately. In calm conditions (no crosswind) such wheels can be an advantage. But for most riders they are prohibitively expensive, and chances are the riders you will be competing against won't be using them, so it's really an unfair advantage. It's best to stick to a light set of traditional wheels.

On most time trial courses you'll want a six-speed, straight block freewheel in 13-18. Some riders prefer a seven-speed 12-18 while others use expensive but light alloy five-speeds.

Aerodynamic clothing

If you've purchased a light set of wheels and still want to make an additional investment in your time trial equipment, Sipay recommends aerodynamic clothing. A good Lycra skinsuit is a fairly sizeable investment but one you should consider. It cuts wind drag to a minimum, especially compared to a wool road jersey with flaring pockets. Lycra has revolutionized not only cycling clothing but also sportswear for swimming, running, and triathlons because it is comfortable, good-looking, and aerodynamic. In just a few seasons it has become the norm in cycling garb.

Some extremely aerodynamic helmets, similar to the Bell model that the U.S. team used in the 1984 Olympics, are currently on the market. The projection on the back of these helmets looks like a pterodactyl's crest but, according to wind tunnel tests, smooths the air flow over your neck and shoulders and can produce a small but measurable advantage. The early helmets of this design were not made to conform to the helmet standards now being mandated by the USCF, but the newer ones use a polystyrene liner and are legal in competition. Check the inside of the helmet to be sure it meets either ANSI Z90.4 or Snell Memorial standards.

Some riders claim that very stiff wooden- or plastic-soled shoes like Duegi or Vittoria help time trial performance. The idea is that all your painfully generated horsepower gets transferred directly to the drive train of the bike instead of getting absorbed in the flex of conventional shoes.

It is a bad idea for most riders to use inflexibly soled shoes just for time trials, while training and road racing in another pair. Different shoes have widely varying shoe and cleat configurations that can lead to knee trouble if you switch them back and forth. Also, wooden soles tend to be a little thicker, effectively changing your saddle height.

So if you want to take advantage of stiffer soles you'll have to put up with their disadvantages – which are the flip side of their benefits – all the time. One of these is that the wood sole is hard and unyielding. Unless it happens to conform exactly to your foot, you'll soon be tempted to get off the bike, sit by the side of the road, and carve the offending wooden ridge out of the sole with a knife. Even if the sole is a good fit with your sole, you can still get numb, burning feet from the pressure. Some manufacturers solve this problem with a cork insole over the wood. You can also use a Spenco insole but you'll pay for the comfort with some give when you pedal, an even thicker sole, and the necessity for a larger shoe to accommodate the insole. Also, wooden soles are reputed to warp if you wear them too often in the rain although quite a few wet-weather riders claim that this isn't a problem.

I have ridden in wooden-soled Duegis for several seasons now and find them comfortable and efficient. Other riders hate such extremes of stiffness. If you are interested in trying out the concept of more power through less sole flex, you'll just have to buy a pair and take a chance on a $70 mistake. But remember, if the shoe isn't comfortable in the shop, it will be less so on the bike. Wooden soles don't break in – they break you.

Other modifications

Some time trialists remove the front derailleur, the inner chainring, and the shift lever and cable to convert the bike to a six speed for use on flat courses. The only drawback here, besides the time involved, is the danger of the chain coming off the chainring since it is no longer guided by the front derailleur cage. Sipay has come up with a cheap chain guide to solve the problem. He recommends putting a slightly oversized light-alloy radiator clamp on the seat tube where the derailleur goes. Run a bolt through the protruding tail of the clamp so that the threaded end of the bolt protrudes out over the top of the chainring. He argues that the chain will unship only if it lifts up and the little bolt will prevent this while adding negligible wind resistance and weight.

An expensive but effective modification is to change to cranks that are 2.5mm longer than your normal ones. This will give you more leverage for pushing bigger gears. The disadvantages of long cranks are that they reduce your ability to spin fast and they give you less clearance when you pedal through a tight corner. But these factors don't matter much in time trials. Don't jump up more than 2.5mm though. Casebeer says, "I use 172.5mm cranks for criteriums, 175s for time trials. This makes it easy to switch between road and time trials because if I rode 180s [for time trials] I'd have a long period of readjustment."

Some riders have a special bike that they use only for TT competition. These don't need to be expensive either. Casebeer proclaims, "Don't feel that if it isn't European it's no good. You can modify lots of good, basic equipment with a little work that will outperform this other equipment, usually at half the price. My time trial bike is 15 pounds and has only one trick piece – a titanium bottom bracket. It is stiff, light, and cost me $500 retail to build. Not bad for a trick bike."

Of course, you can go all the way. Because of the publicity that small-wheeled, so-called "funny" bikes have received in the last several years, they are now available, for a price, at your local shop – 24-inch wheels, cowhorn bars, flattened spokes, gossamer tires, the works. If you can afford to spend the money for such high-tech wizardry, it may even be worth it. There is certainly a psychological boost here. Haserot thinks that "the primary advantage of riding aero equipment is the feeling that you are doing everything you can to enhance your time."

But beware. If you pull out all the stops on equipment, fork over big bucks for a copy of Moser's hour record bike, and still get stomped by some guy riding road wheels on a bike with a pump, spare, and water-bottle cage, the psychological boost will turn into clinical depression. As they say, you pays your money and takes your chances.

Routine maintenance starts with keeping the bike clean. These riders would find their job easier with a workstand.

25
Maintenance

*With a workstand, simple cleaning
and checking takes only 5 minutes*

NO MATTER what kind of equipment you race on, keep it clean and well-adjusted. You don't have to be a great bike mechanic to ride and race nor is there a need to buy the specialized tools or acquire the expertise to face bottom brackets or build wheels. Even such routine maintenance as repacking the bearings in hubs or adjusting the headset can be left to a local shop, although most riders quickly develop these basic skills because it is more convenient.

But real or fancied lack of mechanical ability is no reason to ride a dirty or badly adjusted bike. When he was national team mechanic Sipay would carefully examine the bikes brought to the Olympic Training Center by outstanding riders who attend the camps there. "We can tell if a rider is responsible just by looking at his bike," he says. "It reflects him personally and adds to the air of professionalism."

Basic bike maintenance is relatively easy and takes little time. What follows is an approach that will keep your bike looking new longer, enhance your riding pleasure, and pay dividends in performance and safety.

Get a workstand

I suggest that you invest in a workstand to make cleaning and routine maintenance easier. I used to hang my bike by the bars and saddle from hooks in my garage to clean it after rides but the work area was badly lit and cold except in summer. As a result I cleaned the bike only when absolutely necessary. Now it can be told: I used to be a bike slob. My chain was gunky, the jockey wheel squeaked at inopportune times, and the handlebar tape was so frayed it streamed in the wind.

Since then I've reformed and now I clean my bike after every ride. Well, almost every ride. And the major reason for this dramatic transformation in habits was the purchase of a $35 portable work-stand. It sits on a piece of clear plastic runner in a downstairs room. When I wheel in the bike after a ride I stick it up on the stand. Later it is handy to wipe down with a wet cloth, clean the chain, and spray a little lemon furniture wax on the frame. My bike doesn't always go fast but it smells good. The room has adequate lighting so I can notice any cuts in the tire tread, cracks in the frame, worn cables, or paint chips.

Since the stand is portable, I can take it to races so I can change wheels easily and adjust brakes and derailleur in case they have gotten bumped in transport. I also use it outside the door of motels to make post-race cleaning and maintenance easier. It is a good investment, especially when you consider that my bikes and components last longer because they don't look like they've been used for cyclocross.

Clean and lubricate

Routine maintenance is easy. First keep the bike clean. After all sloppy rides or periodically in dry weather wash your bike thoroughly. Avoid a strong stream of water that may penetrate the bearings. Rinse off the worst of the grime with a garden hose without the nozzle. Use dishwashing soap, warm water, and a sponge to clean the frame and all components to get rid of road grime and dried sweat on the top tube and stem as well as the dried, sticky remains of whatever you had in your water bottle. This often collects around the bottom bracket and cable guides.

Sponge off the tires to get the sand and grit off the casing and at the same time inspect the tread for cuts and the rims for cracks. Sipay likes to wax the frame once a month to make it easier to clean. He also touches up all chips in the paint to eliminate rust spots that could weaken the thin tubing. This is a good time to check the frame for cracks. Inspect the area around the lower head lugs, the brake bridge, the fork blades inside the fork just below the crown, and the chainstays where they touch the bottom bracket. Bright light makes visual inspection easier, so do it in sunlight not in a poorly lit work area.

Next, clean and lube the drive train which is the most important part of the bike to maintain. If you neglect this chore, the lubrication on the chain makes an abrasive paste with dirt and grinds away at chainrings and freewheels. You can rotate several chains so that whenever one gets dirty you always have a clean one to stick on the bike. Several chains rotated equally on your race and training wheels will prevent annoying chainskip when you go from one to the other.

To clean chains, use two solvent containers filled with kerosene or mineral spirits. Soak your chain in one, shaking it around so the solvent dislodges the caked-on build-up. Then scrub the chain with a brush. Many riders use an old toothbrush. When the outside of the chain is clean, dip it in the second solvent bath to get grit out of the inside of the rollers. Then shake the excess solvent off the chain and hang it up to drip dry.

To lubricate, spray with a commerical chain lube like Triflon or Bullshot. Spray it on the mounted chain a few links at a time while you rotate the cranks backward. Then hold a rag over the chain and back-pedal to get the lubricant off the surface. Every couple of rides, spray the chain with WD-40 as a solvent, wipe it down, and relubricate. This seems to work fine between more formal cleanings and rotations of the chains.

When you clean the chain be sure to wipe down the chainrings, derailleur jockey wheel, and freewheel cogs or their dirt will foul the newly cleaned chain.

Wheels and tires

Wheels and tires are the next maintenance priority. True your wheels about once a week because if you ride on a rim with a slight wobble, the rim will become permanently crooked. Avoid unnecessary jumping of your bike over obstructions because when you land, you may flatten the rim slightly.

Proper gluing of tires is crucial or they will roll off the rim in a corner or at the turnaround. Prepare a new rim by cleaning it thoroughly with solvent to remove oil and grease left during manufacture or shipping. Some mechanics score the surface of the rim with a file to roughen it up so the glue has a better surface to adhere to. Apply a smooth base coat of glue, spreading it out with your fingers, and let it dry several days. If you have ferruled rims, get some glue around each ferrule so you have a smooth base.

Prepare new tubular tires by stretching them on a clean rim before they are used. Always mount a new tire without glue on a clean rim and inflate it before you use it. If it is defective you can take it back for a refund but shops won't accept a tire once it has been glued. Age tires by storing them on rims in a cool, dark place preferably for a year or so. Properly aged tires have harder tread that flicks away puncture-causing debris rather than picking it up. A tire aged for a year or so is about right.

When you are ready to mount a tire, inflate it slightly and scrape the latex off the base tape with a dull knife so the glue will adhere better. Apply a fresh coat of glue to the rim and another, thinner coat to the base strip on the tire. Spread it out carefully and allow both surfaces to dry until they are slightly tacky. Stretch the tire on the rim, starting with the valve. Put the wheel on the floor, valve hole up, and press the tire on all the way around until you get to the end. Then flip the tire the rest of the way on with your thumb.

Try to align the tire so that the base tape is equally exposed all the way around. If the tire is still not true when you rotate it, make small adjustments with light pressure in the tire. If you smeared some glue on the rim, clean it with solvent. Inflate the tire to 70 or 80 pounds.

Inspect the tread and sidewalls frequently. If you find cuts, fill them with liquid rubber or the shoe sole repair that runners use. If a pebble hits a minor cut in the tread, its sharp edges can penetrate to the tube or cut the casing threads.

You should coat the sidewalls of new tires with liquid latex solution, available in bike shops, to protect the casing material. Repeat this procedure whenever the coating wears thin or the base tape starts to peel away from the tire. If the latex is still sticky the day after you put it on, sprinkle a little baby powder on it.

Careful inspection

Every four to six months tear apart your hubs, headset, and bottom bracket and repack them. If the bearings are dull, replace them with new ones. Re-tighten your crankarms every 25 miles for the first 100 after you have taken them off. If they work loose the alloy can be ruined by the harder steel of the spindle. Headsets take a beating from road bumps. It is usually the lower race that wears out, so check it each time you repack the bearings and replace it if necessary. A worn or badly adjusted headset can cause shimmy at high speeds and make your bike hard to handle. Re-lube pedals once a year and inspect the spindle carefully.

Inspect brake cables every week or so. They usually wear at the lever end so squeeze the lever and look inside for signs of fraying.

When you replace the rubber brake-lever hoods, look carefully at the brake-lever housing to see if it has cracked around the fixing bolt. You don't want that lever coming off when your weight is thrown forward onto it in an abrupt stop. Preserve the rubber in the hoods by spraying it with Armour-All.

Inspect your toestraps and also the toeclips for cracks around the fixing bolts. Replace all these relatively inexpensive parts frequently to avoid frustrating breakdowns.

With a decent work area and workstand most of these checks and simple cleaning can be done in five minutes after a ride.

*Experienced cyclists who want to train for triathlons should shorten their cycling work-
outs and spend more time running and swimming. But be careful. Your running muscles may not be as ready for these new demands as your cardiovascular system.*

26
Triathlons

How to budget your time and energy
for three sports at once

IF YOU ARE a cyclist thinking about entering a triathlon, you
have a lot to look forward to. Your cycling ability will put you at
an immediate advantage. That's because the cycling leg of the typical swim-bike-run event is usually the longest part, both in time
and distance. And most of the people around you will have come to
the sport from swimming or running.

Because the bike leg of the triathlon is basically a time trial, most
of the information in this book can be used to improve your performance. Both the triathlete and the cycling time trialist must employ a good aerodynamic position on the bike, choose lightweight
but reliable equipment, and use sound training principles such as
periodization and the hard-day, easy-day routine (stress adaptation).

There are a few obvious differences between the time trial and the
triathlon. In competition, assuming the typical swim-bike-run sequence, the intensity of cycling effort is less in a triathlon because
you have to save energy for the run. In training you must budget
time for swimming and running. In technique, the transition
(where you change from one sport to another) replaces the start,
turnaround, and finish of the traditional time trial.

It is worth mentioning that despite the many claims made for the
cross-training approach, which says that doing one sport may help
your performance in another, it is not likely that your time trialing
ability will improve through triathlon training. If you hope to perform at a high level in cycling, specificity of training is best. This
is why most coaches have their athletes use all their available time
to concentrate on a single sport.

This chapter was written by Geoff Drake, an editor at Velo-news,
who is also a racing cyclist and triathlete.

However, the benefits you can realize from cross-training are many, such as reduced risk of injuries and the development of full-body strength. Triathlon training can also relieve the boredom and staleness that sometimes result from emphasizing a single sport. Conversely, an experienced triathlete can certainly benefit from an occasional attempt at a cycling time trial. Perhaps the most famous cyclist-turned-triathlete is John Howard. He is a former USCF national champion (road and time trial), '71 Pan Am Games road champion, and several times Olympic team member who in 1981 won the world's most famous triathlon, the Ironman in Hawaii. Howard recommends time trials for triathletes as a way to increase speed.

Training

The concept of periodization as outlined in this book is a good approach to any sport, including the triathlon. Many cycling coaches recommend a variety of sports during the winter as a pleasant diversion and to promote full-body strength. For the cyclist interested in triathlons, this prescription is easily filled – spend your time in the pool and putting in running miles. Especially if you are an experienced cyclist, winter can be the time to make great gains in these two other sports during a period when you wouldn't be riding that much anyway. If you're not sure you want to devote yourself to triathlons, this will give you the opportunity to try out the training that's involved without serious consequences to your cycling performance later on.

That doesn't mean you should neglect the bike entirely during the off-season. Twice weekly WLS workouts are still a good idea for riders in a cold climate, as are easy road rides for riders in warmer regions. But proceed with the old maxim in mind: Race your strengths, and train your weaknesses. If you are an experienced cyclist, use this time to improve performance in the other two sports.

Running

It goes without saying that if you are inexperienced in running or swimming you should proceed with caution in those sports. Follow the 10% rule, avoiding radical jumps in weekly mileage which exceed that amount. This can be more difficult than it sounds. Cyclists with years of training often have the aerobic power to really do some damage to themselves when taking on a new sport, particularly running. Howard calls this "a combination of ignorance and enthusiasm." When left unchecked, it can sideline you for the season. Don't forget that your running and swimming muscles may not be on the same level as your cardiovascular system when you start out. An initial run of five miles may feel good when you're doing it but you'll pay the next day with sore quadriceps or worse.

One running injury which is a virtual litmus test of excessive jumps in mileage is shin splints, that aching feeling on the inside or front of your calves which signifies a muscle being pulled away from the bone. In one of his first triathlons, Howard suffered a severe case of shin splints which later developed into a stress fracture. If you get shin pain, back off. If it doesn't go away, see a sports physician. Preventive measures include calf stretches, deep massage, and toe lifts.

Don't run in basketball shoes. While a cyclist can compete perfectly well on an inexpensive bike, inexpensive or discount running shoes will only lead to trouble. Find a pair of quality training shoes with good cushioning. If you feel there is anything unusual about your running style, ask a qualified salesman to recommend a special shoe. Be prepared to replace your shoes at regular intervals as they wear.

Work your way up to 15 to 25 miles per week in your running program. Your goal for the spring should be to compete in a short-distance event (typically a one-mile swim, 25-mile bike, and 10K run) rather than an Ironman-distance event, and this type of early season mileage should be sufficient.

Swimming

While much has been said about the importance of technique in cycling, it would be difficult to imagine a sport in which it is more important than swimming. Simple observation proves this. Stand back and watch the swimmers in the fast lane. Those going fastest will be hard to recognize at first. That's because of a complete lack of splashing or jerky movements. They simply glide.

While you might find you look more like a baby whale in the pool, there's hope. It's true that some people benefit from a natural ability to sense resistance in the water, but this gift would never become apparent without endless yards in the pool under the watchful eye of a good coach. The angle at which the arm leaves and enters the water, body rotation, follow-through – all these combine to form a smooth, efficient stroke, and can only be recognized and developed by a competent coach.

If coaching is not available in the form of a swim team or other local program, try asking the lifeguard for advice. While not every lifeguard is a good coach, most will probably know a fair amount about swimming. And their time and advice are free.

Start your swimming program with a trip to the store to buy some goggles. Don't even try swimming in a pool without them.

Initially, you should start out with a mileage base in swimming just as you would at the beginning of the cycling season. Work up to a non-stop quarter-mile distance, and progress to a complete mile. Eventually your swim training will consist mostly of shorter, more intensive efforts, but in the beginning the goal is just to swim a fixed distance without stopping.

After you have achieved proper technique and can swim a mile without difficulty, you should begin experimenting with speedwork, doing several repeats of 50-250 yards. Even during these hard efforts, you should not allow yourself to lose form.

Don't be afraid to include a comparatively high amount of speedwork in your swimming program as the months progress. Recovery occurs quickly in swimming.

Weight training

Many triathletes supplement their program with weight training during the off-season. You should do the same if you have time. Strength training can improve swimming performance dramatically, and most top swimmers spend a lot of time in the weight room. When designing your workout, place special emphasis on upper-body movements such as lat pull-downs, and arm and chest movements, rather than a predominance of heavy lower-body work. Circuit training is popular with triathletes because so many different muscles are used, just as in the triathlon itself.

Hank Lange, professional triathlete and former national cross-country ski coach, cautions against sacrificing too much pool time to weight training. "Many beginners find they feel weak in the pool at first, but they are mistaking inefficient technique for a lack of strength."

As spring approaches many triathletes find they no longer have time for weight training because they are spending more time cycling, running, and swimming. If you do continue weight training it should be a light maintenance program which won't take too much away from your efforts in the other three sports.

The weekly program

If you have been participating in all three sports during the winter, you should have a good aerobic base that will enable you to gradually increase the intensity of your workouts without risking injury. This base is particularly important in the triathlon because time limitations dictate that much of your training be done at a fairly high intensity. Without a good base (and proper warmup), injury will result. But once your aerobic base is established, it's time to progress to a planned weekly schedule that will carry you through the season.

Two factors will influence the design of your weekly program. First, you should decide how much time you have to devote to triathlon training. You can complete a short-distance event on an average of one to two hours of training each day. The other factor is your relative ability in the three sports. If you are a poor swimmer you should be swimming five or six days each week, if possible. If your running is not what it might be, you should try to run four times (always allowing for sufficient recovery).

What about cycling? If you are an experienced cyclist, you should be devoting most of your time to the other two sports. As a result your bike sessions should be fairly short and intense, designed to accomplish the maximum work in the shortest amount of time. Intervals, test TTs (without a standing start), and random jams are all good for the development of pure speed. Take at least one easy ride each week for recovery and to enjoy the bike. In a typical program designed for a short triathlon you might ride a total of three times each week.

Since cycling workouts take longest, you may want to give these workouts their own day. Swimming and running workouts take about 45 minutes, and doing both of those sports in one day is not that much of a burden on your time. Another time-saving trick is to combine workouts by riding to the pool for a swim.

Here is a sample program, based on a total training time of about 12 hours each week accomplished in 13 sessions. Total training time for each weekday is between one and a half and two hours.

Monday: Run three miles easy, swim 3 x 500 yards easy.

Tuesday: Ride 10 miles at race pace, 20 miles total with warmup and cool-down. Swim 3 x 500 yards hard.

Wednesday: Run 6 miles steady, swim 3 x 500 yards steady.

Thursday: Ride intervals, 25 miles total with warmup and cool-down.

Friday: Ride to pool easy, 20 miles total. Swim 1,800 yards easy.

Saturday: Run five hard repeats of 200 to 400 yards, three miles total. Swim 10 x 100 yards hard.

Sunday: Run 8 miles, swim race distance or in open water.

Total distances for week: swimming, 9,000 yards; cycling, 65 miles; running, 20 miles.

As race time approaches, it's a good idea to try a practice triathlon or two, so you know how your body will react to the swim-bike and bike-run transitions. This can also act as a confidence builder before the race. Get up early, swim one mile, cycle 10, and run four. Use your race-day equipment and perform the transitions as if you were racing. Go at about 80% effort.

Clothing

What special equipment do you need for the triathlon? The same bike that will take you to your best performance in a time trial is right for the triathlon. What is different is what you wear. For short- or medium-distance events, many triathletes use one-piece, sleeveless triathlon suits with quick-drying chamois. Wearing the same suit for the whole event saves times in the transitions. In longer triathlons, such as the Hawaii Ironman (2.4-mile swim, 112-mile bike, 26.2-mile run), competitors usually choose to make a complete change into cycling and running gear to be as comfortable as possible.

Another possibility − one used often by Ironman winner Scott Tinley − is to simply wear a swimsuit for the entire event, without bothering to add as much as a T-shirt for the other two events. Obviously, this solution could have painful consequences if you crash. A variation would be to wear a swimsuit for the entire event, adding cycling shorts at the first transition, then taking off your cycling shorts and putting on running shorts at the second transition. Yet another solution is to wear cycling shorts throughout (roll them up for the swim to reduce drag).

One way to avoid having to tie shoelaces is to install lace-locks. These are cylinders which slide over the laces and make tightening as easy as the push of a button.

Whatever clothing you use, it's a good idea to lay it all out the night before the race and practice your changing routine. There is nothing worse than cruising into the transition area, emptying out the contents of your clothing bag, and discovering you forgot your socks.

Racing

One of the most obvious differences between the cycling portion of a triathlon and the cycling time trial is the level of exertion that each requires. In a cycling time trial you cross your anaerobic threshold once as you charge off the starting line, continually flirt with oxygen debt during the miles that follow, and just about expire as you hit the finish. Needless to say, this doesn't work very well for triathlons.

That's not to say the triathlon shouldn't hurt or doesn't require your best effort. It does. But in the typical triathlon the bike portion is second and the run last. In order to complete the run you will have to use careful pacing and change your start and finish techniques on the bike.

When you emerge from the swim leg, chances are that you will be cold and prone to cramping, particularly in the legs. Most people find this is a good time to use a high spin and stay light on the pedals, allowing the blood to redistribute itself to your cycling muscles. It may take three to five miles before you feel you can really apply yourself to the task of riding the bike. This is also a good time to take food and water if you need it.

Riders who are particularly prone to cramping may want to do a quick hamstring stretch in the transition area by hoisting a foot on top of the saddle and leaning forward. A calf stretch can be accomplished while riding by standing and pressing the heel down once you are strapped into the pedals.

The middle of the cycling leg is the time to really apply yourself. If you are an experienced cyclist, the chances are good that you will be able to focus in on the riders ahead of you and advance one by one through the pack. Although your effort must be slightly lower than what you would use in the typical cycling time trial, most other aspects of TT riding come into play here. Use an aerodynamic position as much as possible, pick out the smoothest part of the road, and stand up and accelerate over brief rises to maintain your pace.

Despite rules against drafting in triathlons, riders still seem to move in packs, keeping only the minimum allowable distance between themselves. If you want to shed yourself of these hangers-on you can try a brief attack as you would in a road race. Be sure to pull wide and pass quickly to avoid a penalty or disqualification.

While some TT specialists don't drink water for any length event, it would be a mistake to try that in the triathlon. Do yourself a favor for the run and drink as much as you can during the bike leg. Some people find they can't eat on the bike without getting cramps during the run. You'll have to experiment to find what works best for you.

Your practice triathlons should have given you some idea of how your legs react to idea of running after a hard effort on the bike. Most triathletes ease off the pedals slightly and spin for the last few miles of the bike leg. Even if you have done this, the first few steps of the run will be awkward. Don't expect to knock off your first running mile at a six-minute pace. Just as with the swim-bike transition, your blood must be redistributed to a new set of muscles, and it may take awhile to get your legs under you.

If you have been going head-to-head with someone for most of the bike segment you may be reluctant to ease off before the run because of the risk of being passed before the transition. Consider the easy miles a race tactic — if it works, your fresh legs will enable you take back the lead in the first few miles of the run.

After you have competed in your first triathlon, assess your performance and try to implement the information into your training program. Where were you strongest? Weakest? Should you have drunk or eaten more? Only through careful analysis and planning will you be able to improve your performance in the triathlon, perhaps even moving towards the longer events if that is your goal.

Governing bodies

THE U.S. CYCLING FEDERATION, a not-for-profit corporation founded in 1920, is the national governing body of cycling of the U.S. Olympic Committee and is an affiliated member of the Federation Internationale Amateur de Cyclisme, which is the amateur arm of the world governing body of bicycle racing. The USCF is also allied with the International Human Powered Vehicle Association and the National Off-Road Bicycling Association.

Among the USCF's functions are the establishment and enforcement of racing rules, the sanctioning of events and the licensing of competitors. Even first-time racers must have a USCF license to ride in a sanctioned event, unless the program includes a race for novices. The annual fee is $28 except for Juniors 9-13 who pay $12 (1985 rates). Licensed riders are sent a copy of the USCF rule book and issues of the federation's monthly publication, *Cycling USA*.

The USCF classifies riders by sex and by their age. The classes (one for men, another for women) are as follows: Junior 9-11, Junior 12-13, Junior 14-15, Junior 16-17, Senior 18-19, Senior 20-24, Senior 25-29, Senior 30-34, and so on in increments of five years.

The Senior men class is by far the largest and it is subdivided into four categories based on ability and experience. A first-time license holder aged 18 or older will be placed in Senior Category IV and must remain there until earning the right to upgrade to Category III. This is accomplished by placing in the top three in three qualifying road events, in the top six in six, or simply by competing in eight or more sanctioned races. A Senior Category I is an elite racer with the potential to be on national teams and represent the U.S. in foreign competition.

A license application can be requested by writing to the USCF, 1750 East Boulder St., Colorado Springs, CO 80909. Include $1 if you would like a rule book so you can learn more about the organization of the sport and how races are structured.

The governing body of professional racing in the U.S. is the U.S. Professional Cycling Federation (USPRO). It is affiliated with the

Federation Internationale Cyclisme du Professional, the professional arm of the world governing body of cycling.

USPRO issues licenses which permit individuals to compete as professionals in races sanctioned by pro governing bodies and which are not restricted to amateurs. The USPRO annual license fee is $50 (as of 1984). In addition, USPRO issues race permits and provides for professional team affiliation and sponsorships. A license application and further information may be requested by writing USPRO, RD 1 Box 130, New Tripoli, PA 18066.

Time trial rules

HERE ARE THE RULES for time trial competition from the 1986 rule book of the U.S. Cycling Federation. They are found in the section on racing rules, in part two, which deals with road racing. There is also a chart of time penalties, not reproduced here.

2E. INDIVIDUAL TIME TRIAL.

2E1. Courses may be out and back, around a circuit, or one way. Only out and back and circuit courses may be used for record purposes. A one-time out and back course or a circuit large enough for a single lap is ideal.

2E2. Road bicycles shall be used. Bicycles with a front hand brake and fixed wheel may also be used.

2E3. Starting times shall be at equal intervals, normally one minute.

2E4. Starting order may be chosen by random selection, by numeric order, by seeding (fastest last), or in stage races by inverse order of general classification.

2E5. If a rider appears later than the appointed starting time, the start will be allowed only if it does not interfere with other riders starting on schedule. If it does interfere, the rider may be further delayed. In case of a late start, the appointed time shall be used in computing the results.

2E6. The start sheet with starting order and appointed starting times should be available for riders' perusal at least one hour before start.

2E7. The rider shall be held by an official at the start, but shall neither be restrained nor pushed.

2E8. On an out and back course, riders must stay to the right of the center line at all times. Failure to do so will result in disqualification.

2E9. No rider shall take pace behind another rider closer than 25 meters (80 feet) ahead, or 2 meters (7 feet) to the side. A rider who is observed taking pace shall receive a time penalty as specified in Table 1.

2E10. No restarts are permitted. In a stage race, a rider who suffers a mishap and does not finish may be assigned the time of the slowest rider who finishes. Alternatively, following vehicles may be permitted at the discretion of the chief referee. Any such vehicle must contain a referee.

2F. TEAM TIME TRIAL.

2F1. Teams may be made up of two or more riders. The distance, timing basis, and number of riders who are required to finish must be specified in the official race announcement. Times may be based on any specified finishing position or on the sum of the times of any specified finishers.

2F2. Courses may be out and back, around a circuit, or one way. Only out and back and circuit courses may be used for record purposes. A one-time out and back course or a circuit large enough for a single lap is ideal.

2F3. Only road bicycles shall be used.

2F4. The starting interval between teams will normally be at least two minutes, but may be increased according to the course.

2F5. Starting order may be chosen by random selection, by numeric order, by seeding (fastest last), or in stage races by inverse order of team general classification.

2F6. If a team appears later than the appointed starting time, the start shall be allowed only if it does not interfere with other teams starting on schedule. If it does interfere, the team may be further delayed. In case of a late start, the appointed time shall be used in computing results.

2F7. The riders from each team shall line up side by side at the start. All riders shall be held by officials at the start and shall neither be restrained nor pushed. When there are too few holders, all riders must start with one foot on the ground. All teams must start in the same manner. No restarts shall be permitted for any reason.

2F8. In championship events, teams shall consist of four riders and the team time is the time of the third rider. Thus, at least three riders must finish.

2F9. Teammates on different laps may not work together (entire team disqualified).

2F10. All pushing of riders is forbidden, even among teammates. Such pushing will result in the entire team being disqualified.

2F11. No team shall take pace behind another team closer than 25 meters (80 feet) ahead, or 2 meters (7 feet) to the side (time penalties in Table 1).

2F12. The exchange of food, drink, minor repair items, help with repairs and exchange of wheels or bicycles shall be permitted solely among members of the same team.

2F13. Each team may be followed by a car having no more than four people aboard: a driver and a referee in the front seat and possibly a coach and a mechanic in back. The car may carry up to four bicycles ready for use in case of a mishap. This car may also carry spare wheels and repair material.

2F14. Follow cars shall not be allowed in front of the team but must remain at least 20 meters (65 feet) behind the third rider and must not pass the fourth rider until there is a 75 meters gap between the third and fourth riders, or until the referee decides that it is safe.

Other bicycle racing books from Velo-news

- **The Two-wheeled Athlete,** *Physiology for the cyclist,* by Ed Burke. 36 chapters of practical advice and scientific theory on cycling training, racing, sportsmedicine and nutrition. Will help cyclists, triathletes and athletes from other sports understand and improve their performance. 144 pages, $10.95.
- **Bicycle Road Racing,** *The complete program for training and competition,* by Edward Borysewicz. The complete road racing program of National Coaching Director Eddie Borysewicz, covering all aspects of the major events: road race, criterium, time trial, team time trial and stage race. 288 pages, $22.50.
- **Beginning Bicycle Racing,** *Fast riding for fitness and competition,* by Fred Matheny. Includes training methods, road racing skills and tactics, criterium and time trial technique. Also chapters on equipment, stress, and other information valuable to beginners and experienced riders. 224 pages, $12.95.
- **Inside the Cyclist,** *Physiology for the two-wheeled athlete,* by Ed Burke and others. 30 information-packed articles on bicycle training and competition. Sections include: physiology concepts, training, nutrition and injuries. Illustrated with photos, drawings, graphs, and tables. 160 pages, $9.95.
- **Cyclist's Training Diary.** Not dated, good for any year. 52 one-week segments, each week includes 7 daily entries, a race entry and a weekly summary, plus 12 pages of monthly summaries. Spiral bound for easy use. 192 pages, $7.95.
- **Ten Years of Championship Bicycle Racing.** A record of the most important national and international results from 1972-81. Includes biographies of 10 top U.S. riders of the decade, a year-by-year history of the developments in the U.S. sport, with more than 100 photos by two of the best known cycling photographers in the world. 128 pages, $14.95/ $5.00 clearance.